MAKING MONEY FROM HOME

Make Money Online From the Comfort of Your Home

By

PAUL D. KINGS

DISCLAIMER

© **Copyright 2019 by Paul D. Kings- All rights reserved.**

This document is geared towards providing exact and reliable information in regards to the topic and issue covered. The publication is sold with the idea that the publisher is not required to render accounting, officially permitted, or otherwise, qualified services. If advice is necessary, legal or professional, a practiced individual in the profession should be ordered.

From a Declaration of Principles which was accepted and approved equally by a Committee of the American Bar Association and a Committee of Publishers and Associations.

In no way is it legal to reproduce, duplicate, or transmit any part of this document in either electronic means or in printed format. Recording of this publication is strictly prohibited and any storage of this document is not allowed unless with written permission from the publisher. All rights reserved.

The information provided herein is stated to be truthful and consistent, in that any liability, in terms of inattention or otherwise, by any usage or abuse of any policies, processes, or directions contained within is the solitary and utter responsibility of the recipient reader. Under no circumstances will any legal responsibility or blame be held against the publisher for any reparation, damages, or monetary loss due to the information herein, either directly or indirectly.

Respective authors own all copyrights not held by the publisher.

The information herein is offered for informational purposes solely, and is universal as so. The presentation of the information is without contract or any type of guarantee assurance.

The trademarks that are used are without any consent, and the publication of the trademark is without permission or backing by the trademark owner. All trademarks and brands within this book are for clarifying purposes only and are the owned by the owners themselves, not affiliated with this document.

TABLE OF CONTENTS

Table Of Contents	3
Making Money From Home - Part 1	
Ways To Make Money From Home	10
1. Take surveys online	11
2. Setup a blog	11
3. Rent your car out to those who need it	12
4. Become a freelancer	12
6 Ways to Make Money from Home	14
1. Home/Online Tutoring	14
2. Take Online Surveys	15
3. Affiliate Marketing	15
5. Babysit Kids in Your Home	15
6. Freelance Writing	15
Conclusion	16
How do I earn money from home using the internet?	18
1. Make Money From Home with Online Surveys:	18
2. Make Money From Home with Online Education / Tutoring	19
3. Make Money From Home Blogging	19

    4. Make Money From Home With Youtube and More   20

Making Money From Home Teaching Online Courses   22

    What Are Online Courses?   22

    What Are The Best Websites to Make Money Teaching Online?   23

    What Do I Need To Make Money From Home Teaching?   23

    What Can I Teach Online?   23

    Things You Must Master To Teach Online   23

    So, How Can I Make Money From Home By Teaching Online?   24

    Conclusion   24

Save Money Selling Your iPhone   26

    Sell your iPhone online   26

    Trading your iPhone   27

    Useful tips when selling your iPhone   27

    Backup your iPhone data   27

    Reset your iPhone   28

    Give all the accessories   29

    Conclusion   29

Make Money from Home with Online Surveys   31

    What is an online survey?   31

    How Online Surveys work   31

    Survey Privacy   32

    How can you earn money taking surveys online?   32

Product Testing and Online Surveys 33
How To Find Online Surveys that Pay 33
Doing Your Own Research 34
Conclusion 34

How Much Money Can You Make with Online Surveys? 36

Is completing surveys worth your time? 36
How many surveys panels should you join? 36
Why shouldn't I join to more survey websites? 37
What can you do to earn more with surveys? 37
Time you need to spend on the survey websites 37
What can you do to earn more? 38
How much can you earn from surveys? 39

How Do Online Surveys Work and how to get paid using them 41

How do online surveys work? 41
How to make money online with surveys? 42
Signing up with online surveys websites 42
Should I provide my sensitive information? 43
What happens when you complete the paid survey? 43
How will you get paid? 44

Top Online Survey Sites **46**

1. Savvy Connect 46

- 2. SurveySavvy 46
- 3. MindSwarms 47
- 4. Parent Speak 48
- 5. PineCone Research 48
- 6. Nielsen Digital Voice Research Panel 49

Bad online survey sites that you must refrain from 51
- 1. Toluna 51
- 2. One Poll 52
- 3. Global Test Market 52
- 4. UK My Survey 53
- 5. Pinecone Research 53

Make Money as a Virtual Assistant 56
- Do I need to have experience? 56
- How to become a virtual assistant without any experience? 56
- How do I find my first client? 57
- Offering the services that clients want 57
- Create a portfolio or a website 57
- How to determine your rates 58
- Conclusion 59

Making Money From Home Blogging 61
- Do you want to make money from home blogging? 61
- Monetizing Your Blog 62

What Kind of Commitment Does it Take To Blog ... 62
How Often Should You Blog ... 62
Tips To Help You Write Blog Posts ... 62
Find a Good Name For Your Blog ... 63
Make Your Blog Look Professional ... 63
Conclusion ... 63

How to Make Money with Kindle Books and AMS ... 65

Keep an eye on the popular authors in your genre ... 65
Target the books, which were recently transformed into movies ... 66
Use Amazon Marketing Services (AMS) ... 66
Use negative keywords on AMS ... 67
Use AMS for the reviews ... 67
Take a look at Advertising Outside Amazon ... 67
Resources ... 68
Making Money From Home Selling Stock Photography ... 69

Making Money From Home – Part 2 ... 72

How to Make Money with Kindle Books ... 73

Kindle Money Mastery Review ... 77

Find Profitable Keywords For Your Kindle Books ... 81

Increase Sales of Your Kindle Books ... 85

Make Money with Affiliate Marketing ... 90

Make Money With The Super Affiliate System ... 94

The Freelance Profit Academy Review	100
Make Money With ClickBank	104
Learn How To Generate Traffic To Your Website	108
Make Money From YouTube	112
Making Money From Home – Part 3	116
Make Money from Home with Online Surveys	117
How Much Money Can You Make with Online Surveys?	121
How Do Online Surveys Work and How to Get Paid Using Them	125
Top Online Survey Sites	129
Bad online survey sites that you must refrain from	133
Making Money From Home – Part 4	137
How to Make Money from Home as a Virtual Assistant	138
How to Become a Virtual Assistant (Getting the Skills Needed)	142
How Much Money Does a Virtual Assistant Make	146
What Tasks Virtual Assistants Do To Make Money	150
Top Money Making Virtual Assistant Jobs	154
ABOUT THE AUTHOR	158
Free Gift Offer	160

MAKING MONEY FROM HOME

MAKING MONEY FROM HOME - PART 1

Ways To Make Money From Home

Google records about 250 million people search different ways to make money just like you just did.

Regardless of your status, whether you are a student, or you are working and need to make a little more cash for spending, or you want to make sure you increase the money you have in your savings, with different ways of making money, you will discover your dream will come through.

Here are some ways you can make money from home today:

1. Take surveys online

Until some months ago, I didn't know there were surveys that pay. It's difficult to believe, isn't it? But trust me, this is really correct! When you fill out these surveys, they can fetch you lots of dollars every month.

Whenever there is a qualifying survey, they notify users by email about it; for this reason, I will advise you to sign up for websites that will pay to take surveys, such as [Survey Junkie](), [Swagbucks](), [Vindale Research](), [InboxDollar](), [MyPoints](), and others. When you sign up for any of these websites, you will be allowed to take as many surveys as possible.

2. Setup a blog

If you are very good at writing, this is really a bonus! You can start writing and making money from home simply with this!

A particular paid survey named DollarSprout uses blogging to broadcast information about saving money and also about earning. You can also set up a blog for information broadcast or about anything you think that interest you.

Sign up with Bluehost to get a free domain name and very affordable website hosting.

3. Rent your car out to those who need it

This is a new way you can use to make extra money; when you aren't using your car, you can lend it to people.

Getaround: this is an app that allows you to post your car online for people who are in need of cars to rent; this app automatically connects you with people around you that are in need of a car. Getaround allows renters to book your car directly from the app. When you do this, you can earn extra money.

4. Become a freelancer

One of the best ways of making extra money from home is freelancing; this is because you don't have to invest any of your money before you could start; the only thing you are required to have is a skill people need and will pay you for! You can go into skills like writing, proofreading, graphics designing, creative writing and a lot more. Pick the skills you are good at!!

Sign up with Fiverr and start selling your work today.

MAKING MONEY FROM HOME

6 Ways to Make Money from Home

We all love the idea of earning additional income or leaving our jobs and working from home. We are going to go over 6 Ways to Make Money from Home.

If you think that those who work from home are just scams, think again, because there are many authentic and reliable ways to make money working from home.

No matter what your interest or area of experience, if you have the desire to work from home, someone, somewhere, has a job for you that will require your skills and natural talents. If you are still diligent and flexible, you will find it, and you will not have to spend money on gas or transportation to get to work.

Anyone who has tried to Google to "work at home" or "make money from home" knows that the web is full of different legit sites where you can earn thousands of dollars in the comfort of your living room; but since there's so much of that stuff out there, it can be frustrating to look for legitimate ways to work from home.

Following are some reasonable ideas to consider.

Note: None of them will make you rich overnight, but they are good options to put some extra money in your wallet.

1. Home/Online Tutoring

There is always a need for tutors at any level of education. You can do it at home or find one of the many opportunities to do it online. You can find companies that make finding students easy.

2. Take Online Surveys

There are thousands of online sites that pay to complete surveys, so they can get market data, make sure the site is free! Spend a couple of hours online, and by the weekend you should have made up to a considerable amount of money.

3. Affiliate Marketing

What another way to rake in money? Affiliate marketing gives you a lifetime opportunity of making serious money from the comfort of home by selling other products for a discount. All you need is a Personal computer, stable internet connection, and sound strategies to upsell your products.

To do this job, you need a good voice and personality, and very thick skin; because sometimes it can be hostile. Nonetheless, it is an excellent way to earn income.

Several big companies outsource their cold calling campaigns to third parties who hire domestic workers to make calls. Typically, telemarketers are paid per hour and earn incentives and fees based on performance.

You can use something like Clickbank to make a lot of money.

5. Babysit Kids in Your Home

Many parents are looking for a cheaper alternative to daycare; Consider sitting a couple of children in your home! If you have your children at home, there is the advantage of playing and relating to your children.

6. Freelance Writing

If you have the talent for writing, there are many freelance writer opportunities available, such as writing technical articles or marketing; or articles for magazines, newspapers or magazines.

You can also charge for writing blog articles on various websites, such as the [Yahoo Contributor network](#).

Conclusion

Earning money from the comfort of your home is limitless as there are millions of legitimate ways to make extra cash from home. From Freelancing, taking surveys, working as a virtual assistant, and drop shipping among others.

MAKING MONEY FROM HOME

How do I earn money from home using the internet?

This question originally appeared on Quora: How do I earn money from home using the internet?

There are many ways to make money online. Some ways are free, but some ways you will have to invest either time or money.

Like anything in life, you get what you put into it. If you educate yourself, work hard, paying your dues, so to speak, you can make a lot of money working from home.

My preferred way is affiliate marketing, but here some other good ways to make money from home:

1. Make Money From Home with Online Surveys:

Online surveys are self-administered surveys, conducted through the internet or by mail.

When you fill an online survey, you are provided with an online questionnaire to fill out.

You are asked to provide your opinion on a subject of interest.

Some recommended online survey sites include:

- Survey Junkie
- Swagbucks
- Vindale Research
- InboxDollar
- MyPoints

This is not an exhaustive list. Make sure to check online for reputable companies.

Make sure to check out reviews about these and others on sites like reddit.com.

2. Make Money From Home with Online Education / Tutoring

From the comfort of your home, you can teach someone a topic you are very familiar with.

You could teach students a subject like math. But you can also teach a course online about a professional skill you have learned, such as blogging.

Some popular online teaching services include:

- Udemy.com
- Coursera.org
- Skillshare.com
- Lynda.com

among others.

3. Make Money From Home Blogging

This is one of the easiest and toughest ways to make money online.

Blogging is easy because anyone can write. Even, if you speak a language other than English, you could blog in a foreign language too.

See: Multilingual Blog: Should I Write In English Or My Native Language?

The thing about blogging is that even though it's easy to set up, buying a domain and getting hosting (I recommend using Bluehost or HostGator), there are many things to learn, such as SEO (Search Engine Optimization).

You also need to be consistent, posting content to your blog on a regular schedule.

With blogging, you can earn money with affiliate links (using Amazon Associates, or ClickBank, for example), advertising (using Adsense), and selling your own products (such as Ebooks or online courses).

The reason I recommend paying for your hosting, as mentioned above, is because free sites like Blogger.com constrain what you can do to make money. Buying a domain name and hosting is not expensive. In the end, I think you will be glad you went the paid route.

4. Make Money From Home With Youtube and More

As you may already know, Youtube it's a good source of income. You can do affiliate marketing and make tons of money.

But just like blogging, you need to be consistent when you produce content. You want people to start expecting your videos and see you as an authority in your niche.

Making Money From Home Teaching Online Courses

Would you like to make money from home teaching an online course?

There are many interesting ways to make a living from the comfort of your home, and today we present one of the most interesting methods that have been generating great demand on the web: teaching online courses.

The strong demand for online courses has led to the emergence of a new job market. It is no novelty that technical careers, professions, and master's degrees are offered by these means.

However, what is more striking is the infinite range of possibilities that facilitates teaching and studying.

Teaching an online course is an excellent way to make money from home. Here are some basic ideas on how to start teaching online and being successful.

What Are Online Courses?

Online courses refer to virtual education, meaning everything from instructions, programs, evaluations, and certificates are processed online.

Being a teacher of an online course is not as complicated as it seems. There are several websites that allow you to teach what you know and earn a good commission.

There are other more rigorous platforms that require a qualification process. Those platforms want their teachers to provide a "more professional" service.

What Are The Best Websites to Make Money Teaching Online?

There are so many websites on which you can make money from home teaching online. Some popular online teaching services include Udemy.com, Coursera.org, Skillshare.com, Lynda.com, among others.

You can set up your own website if you have enough people who would like you to teach them.

What Do I Need To Make Money From Home Teaching?

On most of the sites mentioned, you register for free, publish your ad and wait for the students to register. Of course, it is not as simple as it seems.

Do not expect that in the first week you will have a class full of students eager to receive your knowledge. Everything takes time.

What Can I Teach Online?

You can teach online things you're good at, for example, philosophy, technology, languages, programming, web design, cooking, music, etc.

If you want to stand out as a great teacher on your online courses, making money from home, then I recommend you exceed the expectations of the students, working hard in each class.

Things You Must Master To Teach Online

You must master basic practices such as group video calls, chat conversations, slide presentations, and other essential resources for web interaction.

Online courses operate in two modalities: streaming classes (live and direct, with student participation to clear doubts) or video tutorials (classes recorded in units to be played at any time).

So, How Can I Make Money From Home By Teaching Online?

Something you need to consider is the marketing strategies to make you known and generate interest among the virtual communities of students.

Think about subjects you already know and can teach online. Do you think you can make an attractive offer to students? The more specialized your class is, the better chances you will have to attract new students.

Let me give you an example; if you publish a course on "graphic design", you must compete against the thousands of courses that abound in the network related to the subject. On the other hand, if you specialize in "infographic design" classes, the result will be different.

In the second case, your courses will be aimed at a specific audience: programmers, designers, and even architects.

Conclusion

There is a strong demand for online courses. You can certainly make money teaching online. To teach online, you will need to work hard and have patience.

It would surprise you to see how profitable teaching an online course can be. Remember that the more specific knowledge you have, the better the results in quality, teaching, and profits. Good luck!

MAKING MONEY FROM HOME

Save Money Selling Your iPhone

Do you have an iPhone you don't use any longer? Or are you looking forward to selling your existing iPhone and go for a better one?

Several effective methods are available for the iPhone owners out there in the world to sell their devices.

Sell your iPhone online

Going online is the best method available for you to sell your used iPhone in today's world. That's because people in today's world go online when they want to purchase a second-hand iPhone.

Many websites are available for you to consider when you are selling the iPhone. Websites to consider are:

- Craigslist.com
- Recycler.com
- Oodle.com
- Olx.com
- Geebo.com
- Gazelle.com

If you want to sell your iPhone to someone in your country, or in your local area, you can look at the online classifieds websites. These websites are easy to use.

You can publish your advertisement in one of the classified websites and make it visible for the potential buyers. Interested people will contact you.

MAKING MONEY FROM HOME

You will also be able to sell your iPhone online to the customers who come from different parts of the world.

You can look at online marketplaces, such as eBay or Amazon. Create and publish your listing and make the iPhone visible for them.

If the product is sold, you can ship it to the destination and get money to your hand.

Trading your iPhone

Apart from selling your iPhone, you can also think about trading it.

If you are interested in upgrading your iPhone to a newer model, this will be the most convenient method available for you to consider.

You can give your old iPhone and then get a new one by making the balance payment.

Now you must wonder about the places you can trade your iPhone.

Some iPhone sellers in your local area will be interested in trade-ins. You can choose a reputed seller out of them and go forward with one.

The Apple Store is also a place to trade in your iPhone. If you have an Apple Store in your region, you can get in touch with them and ask for more information.

Before you trade in the iPhone, also ask how much money you can get for trading the iPhone.

Then you can use your bargaining power and make sure you end up with the best possible deal.

Useful tips when selling your iPhone

Now you know the best methods available for you to sell your iPhone. There are other useful tips, which you need to keep in mind when selling your iPhone so you can stay away from hassle and frustration.

Backup your iPhone data

After you sell your iPhone, you cannot take any of the data stored in it. Therefore, you need to make a backup of the device.

You can take the backup to your iCloud. Then you can get the information uploaded to the cloud.

You can also choose what items, such as contacts, photos, and messages, which you need to back up to the cloud.

Here are the steps you should follow to take a backup of your iPhone.

- Log into your iCloud account from your iPhone; visit the Settings and tap on your Apple ID.
- You can see all your devices tagged under your Apple ID here. Select the iPhone you are selling from the list.
- Tap on the iCloud Backup option and make sure it is switched on.

Reset your iPhone

Your iPhone has personal and sensitive information about you. You want no one to access them.

That's why you must reset and delete data available in your iPhone before you sell it.

You can learn how to reset my iPhone to sell it and it will help you avoid a lot of hassle and frustration in the future.

Do a hard reset on the iPhone. This will ensure no personal information remains on the phone.

After you verify that no personal information is left, you can give it or ship it to the new owner.

Here are the steps you need to follow to reset your phone.

- Go to Settings in your iPhone.
- Choose "General"
- Scroll to the bottom and select "Reset".
- Next, you need to select "Erase All Content and Settings".

Give all the accessories

When shipping the iPhone to the buyer, include the accessories. The new owner will appreciate that.

Conclusion

If you want to sell your iPhone, there are many options online and offline to do so. There is also an easier way, to trade-in your iPhone for a newer model.

However, selling your phone yourself will result in more money than trading it in.

When selling or trading in your iPhone, wipe your iPhone of any personal data.

Also, ship the iPhone with any accessories you can give the new owner.

Make Money from Home with Online Surveys

If you are looking for a convenient and a hassle-free method to make money from home, learn about online surveys that pay people who take them. You need not have any special skills to make a decent amount of money through online surveys.

Having a basic understanding of how to use computers and how to access the internet will be more than enough to help you achieve positive results.

What is an online survey?

For an easy way to make money working from home, you can do online surveys. Continue reading to get a better understanding of what they are.

You can make a decent amount of money at the comfort of your home doing online surveys.

Online surveys are self-administered surveys, conducted through the internet or by mail. Self-administered surveys differ from administered surveys, which are conducted through telephone or face to face.

How Online Surveys work

When you fill an online survey, you are provided with an online questionnaire to fill out. You are asked to provide your opinion on a subject of interest.

When filling out an online survey, you. You are given more than enough time to provide answers to the questionnaire. All you have to be is honest when you fill the questionnaire, to do justice to the survey and the survey organizer.

In fact, the overall quality of an online survey depends on the information you provide. Because of this reason, I encourage you to provide reliable information when completing the online survey as much as possible.

Survey Privacy

When you complete an online survey, the answers you provide, but not your identity, will be sent to the client. It is possible to aggregate the survey results by combining multiple responses along with the individuals who took part in it.

Read the privacy policy of the survey company you are using to make money from home. For example, see here.

Usually, all the data collected from the questionnaire is stored in a database. When the clients want to gain access to the data, they refer to the database. However, as mentioned earlier, your identity is not provided to the external entity.

Additionally, your identifiable personal data should not be traded or sold without your permission.

How can you earn money taking surveys online?

Now you should have a basic understanding of what online surveys are. With that in mind, it is important to understand how to make money with online surveys. People who conduct surveys are hungry for data.

They are always looking forward to getting in touch with individuals, who can fill the questionnaires and help them with their research activities. Since it is not an easy task to get people to spend their time and fill in lengthy questionnaires, they pay people to take surveys too.

In other words, you spend your time and effort to go through the questions and answer them. For that, they will compensate you with a decent amount of money.

Product Testing and Online Surveys

Online surveys go hand in hand with the product tests. Sometimes, they will provide you with a dummy product to test. You need to use that product and write your honest opinion about it.

You can be paid for testing a product. Therefore, keep that in your mind when you are looking for an effective method on how to make money working from home.

How To Find Online Surveys that Pay

Now you may wonder how to find online surveys that will pay you for taking them. Finding good online surveys to complete is not something difficult to do. That's because many websites gather valuable data about their customers when those customers take online surveys.

As mentioned earlier, some recommended online survey websites are:

- Survey Junkie
- Swagbucks
- Vindale Research
- InboxDollar
- MyPoints

Take a look at those websites and determine which ones you prefer. You should be able to complete surveys according to your specific preferences and make a decent amount of money from home.

The time you spend filling out online surveys from these companies mentioned is worth it since you will be compensated when taking the online surveys.

Doing Your Own Research

To get the most out of filling online surveys and make money working from home, I encourage you to do your own research and learn about the best websites that provide the opportunity to make money filling out online surveys.

Go into forums and read what other users of those survey companies say. Find out if the company is a reputable company, who will actually pay people that take their surveys. Also, see if there are any complaints about these companies.

You can take a look at this article here to find other online surveys and a review about them.

Conclusion

You can make money from home filling out online surveys. Taking online surveys, it's a convenient and a hassle-free way to make money online.

Check out the recommended online survey companies mentioned in this article. Also, find out from other users whether a particular online survey company is reputable and will pay you.

Please leave a comment for an online survey company you recommend.

MAKING MONEY FROM HOME

How Much Money Can You Make with Online Surveys?

Are you about to make money working from home? Then you must be looking for how much money you will be able to earn with it.

It's not possible to give a direct answer to the question how much money you can make with online surveys? That's because the specific amount of money that you can earn vary based on several factors.

Is completing surveys worth your time?

As the first thing, let's see if completing surveys online is worth your time or not. As mentioned earlier, the amount of money you can earn with online surveys will change on a daily basis.

The time you spend on completing online surveys can create a major impact on the specific amount of money that you can earn. Likewise, the nature of surveys can also create an impact on the amount that you can earn.

These factors are within your control. Therefore, you need to take a look at the methods on how you can find surveys, which can help you to earn a decent amount for the time and effort that you spend.

Then you will not end up with any disappointments when completing the surveys online.

How many surveys panels should you join?

Some people believe that joining a lot of survey panels can help them to make money online. However, signing up with more survey websites doesn't mean that you can earn hundreds of dollars per month.

Instead, you will end up with a loaded email box, which is quite overwhelming.

It is recommended for you to go ahead and sign up with around 5 different survey websites. This is the optimum number of panels that you must sign up with in order to make a decent amount of money.

You can begin with 5 panels and see if there is any possibility for you to receive benefits by signing up with more panels in the future. This kind of approach can help you to end up with impressive results in the long run.

Why shouldn't I join to more survey websites?

You need to keep in mind that some of the most prominent survey websites are working with the same market research companies that exist out there in the world.

This is the main reason why you will not be able to increase your chances of making more money, by signing up with more survey websites.

Even if you are invited, you will not be able to complete the survey. That's because the surveys tend to log your IP address to avoid fraud.

What can you do to earn more with surveys?

As you can see, signing up with more survey websites cannot help you with earning more. It is recommended for you to begin with a couple of websites, which are reputed.

Get cash for surveys and Paid surveys are few examples for such websites. You can sign up with these websites and see how they work. Then you can join the other websites and proceed.

Time you need to spend on the survey websites

If you are interested in making a serious amount of money with online survey sites, you will need to invest a considerable amount of time on a daily basis.

There are no shortcuts to earn more while completing surveys. However, the time you spend with them is totally worth when compared to the amount that you can earn at the end of the month.

Most of the people tend to spend around 4 hours a day by completing surveys online. If you can work more hours, you should do it as the chances of making more money will increase.

But if you are working on surveys for more than 8 hours a day, you need to take precautions. It can lead you towards fatigue and headaches.

What can you do to earn more?

Instead of spending several hours on a daily basis to make money with online surveys, you can select around two survey websites and focus on the completion of surveys.

Some people tend to treat the online survey websites as a regular job. When you master the art of completing surveys to make money, you can treat it like your full-time job. Until that, you are encouraged to work on it as your side-hustle.

You can focus on the online surveys during your off days. You can make it a habit to check your emails as the first thing you wake up in the morning.

Then you will be able to see the invitations from the survey websites. Or else, you can directly refer to the survey websites that you have signed up with.

You must always keep in mind that completing surveys should be a fun-filled experienced and it should not lead you towards any stress.

How much can you earn from surveys?

It is not possible to give a direct answer to this question. That's because the exact amount of money you can earn varies from one survey panel to another.

It also varies depending on the surveys that you complete. Some panels tend to make the payments with points whereas others make the payments directly with cash.

Even though the points have a monetary value, it can be quite tricky. Therefore, you need to be aware of it when you are completing online surveys.

The exact amount of money you can earn from a survey depends on the length of the survey and the depth of the survey. You might get $10 from one survey, whereas you will only be provided with $1 on another survey.

However, the survey that you have to do to earn $1 will only take 5 minutes, whereas you will have to spend 1 hour to complete the survey that you have to do to earn $10.

Technically, completing more of $1 surveys is better than you can earn more money at the end of the hour.

MAKING MONEY FROM HOME

How Do Online Surveys Work and How to Get Paid Using Them

Online surveys are one of the most popular methods available for the people to make money working from home. If you are struggling to earn a decent income by working on your spare time, this is a good opportunity available to grab.

All you have to do is to complete the questionnaires at your home and make an earning for it.

Before you start completing online surveys to make money, it is important to have a basic understanding on how they work.

Then you will be able to work accordingly and maximize your chances of making more money.

How do online surveys work?

You will be able to find many websites, which offer online surveys for the interested people to complete.

However, the way how these surveys work differ from one to another. On the other hand, the way how specific surveys are being used also differ from one to another.

In general, the companies and other similar entities are in need of data to make informed decisions about their future initiatives. For example, a company tends to gather customer data before launching a new product.

Then they determine whether the product will be successful among customers. On the other hand, the data a company gathers can also contribute towards making appropriate changes product to make it popular and useful for the potential customers.

Out of data collection methods available for the companies, surveys hold a prominent place. However, no person is willing to spend his precious time and complete the surveys to help the companies.

As a result, the companies tend to make a payment for the people, in favor of completing the questionnaires and providing them with valuable data. This is how the online surveys work.

How to make money online with surveys?

Now you have a basic understanding about the purpose of online surveys. With that in mind, you can take a look at how you will be able to make money working from home with the assistance of online surveys.

You will be answering the questionnaires that the companies provide with the objective of gathering data. You need to be honest when providing answers to them.

Then you need to go ahead and submit your answers. In return, you will be provided with a payment. Completing online surveys is simple as that. You don't need to have any special skills to do it and make money at the comfort of your home.

Signing up with online surveys websites

To begin with, you can sign up with the online survey websites. However, you need to be vigilant at the time of signing up.

That's because there's many scam websites on the internet and you will need to take appropriate measures to stay away from them. You should not sign up with any website that requests for a large upfront fee.

At the time of signing up to a website that provides online surveys, you will have to answer a series of questions. These questions will be about yourself and the lifestyle that you follow.

These questions are asked from you because the website needs to provide you with surveys that match with you.

Therefore, you must be honest when providing answers to these questions. On the other hand, this will help you to get interesting surveys to complete, based on your preferences.

Should I provide my sensitive information?

When you are signing up with online surveys websites to make money working from home, you will have to provide your sensitive information.

They include your name, your address, your email address, your contact number and your age. This is applicable even for the most prominent websites that provide surveys, such as Get Cash for Surveys and Paid Surveys for Cash.

The companies that offer surveys to the websites are looking for the best fitting individuals to complete them.

Otherwise, they will not be able to end up with accurate information. This is the main reason why they ask for your personal and sensitive information.

For example, when you enter your age, you will be provided with surveys that match perfectly well with your age. A teenager would not want to complete a survey about senior care facilities.

If you don't want to end up with such questionnaires, you need to provide your honest information.

You don't need to think twice before you feed your personal information to a reputed website. Your personal and sensitive information is protected at all times. Therefore, you don't need to worry about anything.

What happens when you complete the paid survey?

When you are completing the online survey, you will have to answers to the questions. All the answers that you provide will be submitted to the company that provides the questionnaire.

You are not the only person who completes the survey. All the gathered data will be analyzed by the company that provides the survey.

Then the company will take appropriate measures in order to improve their products, services or the business processes.

The next stage associated with online surveys is quite technical. In fact, the companies are looking forward to finding the cheapest place in order to produce the products or sell the products.

The data that the company gathers from surveys provide a great assistance when making decisions.

However, you need to provide your honest opinion when completing the surveys, so that you will be able to provide assistance for the companies to make better decisions.

How will you get paid?

Some websites that offer online surveys pay with cash, whereas others pay with coins. You can convert the coins to cash at a later stage. When you keep on completing surveys, you will be able to make more money.

Then you will be able to withdraw them to your bank account or any other online wallet such as PayPal.

MAKING MONEY FROM HOME

MAKING MONEY FROM HOME

Top Online Survey Sites

When you want to make money working from home, you can take a look at the paid surveys online. To engage with paid surveys, you must take a look at the websites that provide you with the surveys.

many such websites are available on the internet, but all of them are not in a position to provide you with an excellent service as you expect.

That's why we thought of providing you with a list of the best online surveys websites. If you want to make money online, you can take a look at these websites and you will be able to receive impressive results.

1. Savvy Connect

Savvy Connect is one of the most innovative platforms available for you to complete surveys and get paid for them. To begin with, you will need to install the app on your PC, mobile or any other device, which you can use to connect to the internet.

Then this app will work in the background and gather required information.

To increase your earnings with Savvy Connect, you can recommend it to others. For every person who installs this app, you will be able to earn around $5 to $15.

There is no minimum payout to withdraw and you will be able to receive a check payment upon request.

2. SurveySavvy

SurveySavvy has received a lot of attention in the recent past as well.

That's because the website provides people with access to the highest paying surveys.

You will be able to earn somewhere in between $1 to $20 by completing the surveys available on this website. Therefore, it can be considered as a website that you must use.

SurveySavvy also provides additional payments for the referrals that you bring in. When you bring in more referrals, your chances to make money online will increase.

That's because you will be able to earn in between $1 to $2 for every survey that your referrals complete. Moreover, you can earn around $0.5 to $1 via the indirect referrals as well. No minimum payout is needed for you to request a withdrawal on this website. You will be able to get funds via a check.

3. MindSwarms

Among the online surveys websites, MindSwarms is another highly discussed option available for you to consider. You will be able to complete highly paying surveys, which can provide you with up to $50 per survey on this website.

Therefore, you can engage with it without keeping any doubts or second thoughts in mind. To earn this amount, you will not have to complete lengthy surveys. It is possible for you to complete a survey with just 7 questions and earn $50.

The MindSwarms website has an interactive survey completion mechanism as well. You will be provided with the questions on the interface.

These questions are determined based on your profile and demographics.

You will be provided with 7 such questions to answer on this website.

At the end of the questionnaire, you can receive the payout. MindSwarms makes the payments through PayPal.

4. Parent Speak

Parent Speak is an online surveys website that is available for the parents to use. If you are a parent who is looking forward to make money working from home, you can take a look at this website.

Parent Speak is backed up by C+R Research, which is a marketing firm based in Chicago. This is not just a survey website.

As a parent, you will be able to connect with other parents and discuss many things through this platform.

Most of the surveys that you can find in Parent Speak are linked with follow-up questions. Therefore, it will take a considerable amount of time for you to complete them.

They cover a variety of topics, which are related to the parents, such as clothing, entertainment, food and electronics.

You can earn around $20 to $50 by completing the surveys available on this website. Payments will be made through check.

5. PineCone Research

If you are looking for an exclusive online survey panel, you can take a look at PineCone Research. That's because not all people can sign up for accounts on this website.

You will only be able to create an account in PineCone Research if you are invited. In addition, you need to keep in mind that PineCone

Research has specific quotas for invitations as well.

If the quota is reached, you will not be able to create an account on PineCone Research, even if you have an invitation.

Previously, PineCone Research made a flat rate payment of $3 for every survey that you took.

However, the things have slightly changed now and you will be able to earn more or less depending on the nature of the survey that you take.

You need to have a minimum amount of at least $3 in your account to initiate the withdrawal. Payouts in PineCone Research will be made through Visa gift cards, direct deposits and checks.

6. Nielsen Digital Voice Research Panel

Nielsen Digital Voice Research Panel is a survey website that is backed up by a market research group.

The entire program was developed with the intention of gathering information related to audience size and audio composition of the television programs that are being telecasted in United States.

Now Nielsen Digital Voice Research Panel has increased the scope. As a result, you will be able to discover a lot of additional surveys available in the website.

You can sign up with Nielsen Digital Voice Research Panel for free. Then you need to install the free app that they give to your computer or any other device.

The app will work on the background and collect appropriate data. At the end of every month, you will be able to enter to the $10,000 sweepstakes, where 400 lucky winners walk away with amazing prices.

MAKING MONEY FROM HOME

BAD ONLINE SURVEY SITES THAT YOU MUST REFRAIN FROM

When you want to make money working from home, you tend to take a look at the online surveys websites.

That's because there is a high possibility for you to make a decent amount of money by spending minimum effort.

However, all the survey websites that promote the ability to make money online cannot deliver guaranteed results.

If you are about to complete surveys online, you are encouraged to have a clear understanding about these websites. Then you can take appropriate steps to refrain from those websites.

Here is a list of bad online survey sites that you need to refrain from.

1. Toluna

Toluna is a website that provides you with the opportunity to test products at the comfort of your home and write reviews on them.

However, the rewarding system that you can find on this website is somewhat poor. You will not be compensated enough for the time that you spend in order to complete surveys on this website.

On the other hand, the surveys that you complete on this website aren't worth very much as well.

When you create an account on Toluna, you will notice that your email inbox is getting bombarded with notifications and emails.

These emails don't have any value and it will be a big headache. You will be earning points for the completion of surveys on Toluna.

However, you will need to use those points within a period of one year upon earning. Otherwise, you will lose access to the points.

2. One Poll

One Poll promotes itself as a great little website, which can help you to earn money during your coffee breaks. But when you sign up with this website, you will notice that it is not interesting as it sounds.

You will not be able to earn a lot of money when you complete the surveys. In fact, completion of a survey will only provide you with $0.10 to $0.15.

The time you spend on the work is not worth when compared to the results that you get.

In some surveys that you complete in One Poll, you will be able to receive the rewards as prize draws.

You will not be able to get any money from these surveys. The prize draws don't guarantee monetary prizes to you as well.

Therefore, you might have to walk away with nothing. When you are completing online surveys on this website, you will need to earn at least 40 GBP before you can request for a withdrawal.

With the amount of money that you can make on the site, it will take a considerable amount of time for the withdrawals.

3. Global Test Market

Global Test Market is an established website which you can use to make money through the completion of surveys.

You will be able to get surveys to complete on a daily basis after creating an account on this website. However, most of those surveys are broken. This will make you waste a considerable amount of time when completing them.

Before you start filling the questionnaire, you will have to go through a screening process as well.

This screening process is relatively long and it will take a couple of minutes. Some surveys available on this website will also take ages to complete.

However, you will not be able to receive a decent amount of money for the time you spend to complete them.

Even though Global Test Market records all your personal information at the time of creating the account, you will notice that you are getting completely irrelevant surveys at times.

4. UK My Survey

UK My Survey is a great platform available for the people in UK to complete surveys and make money. However, there are some drawbacks associated with this website as well.

The biggest drawback out of them is constant screen outs. This can lead you towards a lot of frustrating moments when you complete the surveys.

In addition to that, you will be able to discover many broken surveys on the website as well.

You will notice that most of the surveys that are available to complete on this website are similar.

If you ignore this fact and complete the surveys, you will come across issues with the payment. In fact, you will not be able to receive a payment for the duplicate surveys.

5. Pinecone Research

Pinecone Research is another popular online surveys website. If you are looking forward to make money working from home through this website, you need to take a quick look at the drawbacks linked with it.

The entire website has a somewhat confusing design. You will get confused when you are trying to access the reward center.

In fact, you will have to struggle a lot when you are trying to locate the withdrawal button for the very first time when using the website.

You will also be asked to enter your user name and password when you are trying to complete a survey at all times. This can also lead you towards a lot of pain.

Only one person at your home will be allowed to create a Pinecone Research account. The sign-up process is quite complicated as well.

Completion of surveys is the only method available for you to make money on Pinecone Research. There is no friend referral scheme.

Now you are aware of some of the worst online survey websites available on the internet. You must take appropriate steps to stay away from these websites.

If you take a closer look at these websites, you will notice some common aspects in between them as well.

Therefore, you are encouraged to keep your hands away from the online surveys websites that come with such features.

Then you can get the most for the amount that you spend with completing online surveys.

Make Money as a Virtual Assistant

Did you know you can make money working from home as a virtual assistant?

You will be able to provide a service you are familiar with and make a considerable amount of money.

Do I need to have experience?

Even if you are not an expert in a specific area, you can still try to become a virtual assistant. You can catch up, improve your skills, and make money online.

In fact, you will get paid to learn when you are working as a virtual assistant. This will help you to grow your business and improve your chances of making a solid income.

How to become a virtual assistant without any experience?

Making money as a virtual assistant without any experience can be difficult. You are encouraged to do a bit of research on the market before you offer your services.

You can see what other people do as virtual assistants to make money. You can get ideas on what you can or would like to do as a virtual assistant.

One example, you can make money helping someone doing social media management. Or else, you can research on a subject matter and provide recommendations.

You shouldn't aim to make thousands of dollars from the first month you work as a virtual assistant. Instead, you must aim for a slow beginning.

How do I find my first client?

When it comes to freelancing, looking for your first client is the most difficult thing to do. This is applicable for the individuals who make the decision to work as virtual assistants as well. You will not have any idea at all on how to find a client.

In this kind of situation, the freelancing websites can help you with. You can visit freelancing websites such as Fiverr, Freelancer, and Upwork.

In addition, the lesser known websites such as People per Hour can also provide you with impressive results when looking for a virtual assistant. You can find clients who are looking for virtual assistants. You can then offer your services to them.

Offering the services that clients want

Clients want many types of virtual assistant related services. It is better if you can have a basic understanding of those services before you begin. You will be able to make appropriate decisions when applying for jobs online.

The virtual assistants will have to work on freelance writing, Book writing, guest blogging, blog management, marketing campaign management, webinars, social media scheduling, social media management, email management, copywriting, researching, fact-checking and many more.

You can narrow down your focus on a few of these services, especially when you are looking for your very first client. When you gain experience while working as a virtual assistant, you can think about offering more services.

Create a portfolio or a website

If you want to make money as a virtual assistant, you are encouraged to create a portfolio or a website. On the website, you can highlight your previous experiences working as a virtual assistant.

The primary objective of creating a portfolio or a website is to increase your credibility as a virtual assistant. This can contribute a lot towards your future success.

You can also add some packages to your website. You will be able to provide more information to the potential clients, who are willing to get the services that you offer.

In addition, you need to get some client testimonials on your website. You can reach to your previous clients and tell them that you have created a new website and you are looking forward to improving it with some reviews.

Clients can leave reviews about the services that you offered them.

You must also get a contact form for the website that you create. Otherwise, you will miss out a lot of opportunities that are available. The contact form can help potential clients to get in touch with you and hire you for their virtual assistant tasks.

I recommend using a professional hosting company for your website. The first hosting company I recommend is [Bluehost](). This is because Bluehost makes it so easy to create a professional website in minutes.

In addition, Bluehost offers great customer support and a 30-day money-back guarantee.

How to determine your rates

What is the best way to make money as a virtual assistant? It has been identified that most of the virtual assistants get confused when they are determining their rates.

Some virtual assistants tend to charge per hour but others charge a flat rate.

In the beginning, it is better if you can charge your clients on an hourly basis. That's because you will not be able to make a clear estimation of how much time it will consume for you to get the job done.

When you have some experience working as a virtual assistant, you will know how much time it will cost you to get a specific task done. In that kind of situation, you can simply switch to a flat rate.

You will be able to increase the amount of money that you make. However, your rates should be reasonable for the clients.

Conclusion

Now you know how to make money online by working as a virtual assistant. With that in mind, you can go ahead and follow the steps.

It is an easy and a hassle-free method that any person can follow to make a decent amount of money at the comfort of home. You can also keep on learning new skills and it will help you to take your work to the next level.

If you dream of becoming a successful virtual assistant in the future, you are encouraged not to stop learning. You can stay up to date and polish your skill set at all times to deliver a better service to your clients.

MAKING MONEY FROM HOME

MAKING MONEY FROM HOME

Making Money From Home Blogging

You can make money from home blogging this year. Learn about blogging and the money opportunities you have in 2019.

The information in this blog post first appeared on my book "Make Money Blogging: Strategies to Earn Passive Income" found on Amazon and other online bookstores.

Do you want to make money from home blogging?

Blogging is a brilliant way to get out in the online world. Blogging provides an excellent way to get recognition as an expert in your chosen field. Over 175,000 people start a new blog every single day, so you want to start out with the right foot forward to, you know, stay ahead of 'the pack.'

Blogging can be an enjoyable hobby. You get to write about your favorite topics and spark a conversation with other bloggers.

Most people blog to make money. While making money blogging can be difficult to achieve, it can be done with the right amount of work. Before you worry about making money with your blog, set it up first.

Using a free blogging platform such as Blogger is good if you want to try things out first. But for serious blogging, you have to pay for hosting and you have to use WordPress.

I recommend using Bluehost for your hosting company because it provides a one click installation of WordPress and you don't need to fumble around with technical stuff before your blog is live to the world to see.

Monetizing Your Blog

There are many ways you can make money from the comfort of your home with a blog. You can place ads from Google on your blog. They will pay you each time a visitor clicks one of their ads.

You can also get set up with affiliate sites. These sites work well with blogs and pay well. Blogging for money requires a lot of patience and tweaking. To make money blogging, you will need to have sufficient traffic.

What Kind of Commitment Does it Take To Blog

Updating your blog will require a commitment from you. You will need to establish a regular time to search for and write about fresh news and get it posted.

There will be times when there is not much to blog about; and there will be times when you can't type fast enough.

How Often Should You Blog

You should post to your blog two or three times a week. Publish posts, even if it's only to tell your readers that not much has happened. Share your thoughts and tell your readers when you will publish a post next.

Your audience will keep coming back as long as they know you are.

Tips To Help You Write Blog Posts

Keep your blog as simple as you can, without sounding like you don't have a complete grasp on your subject. You want to appeal to as many people as possible.

Nothing will drive those interested in a subject away faster than lots of technical jargon and statistics. You can present complex information as long as you try to put it in user-friendly terms.

Find a Good Name For Your Blog

Find a memorable name for your blog and use your blog editing feature to post its title in large bold-face type.

A blog named "My Hiking Blog" will sound interesting only to Mom and Dad and only because you never write or call them while you are out adventuring.

A blog named "Climbing through the Clouds" will appeal to those who either tackle the high places of the planet or want to.

Make Your Blog Look Professional

Make sure your blog looks professional. You have a spell checker, so use it. Proofread your copy and correct any grammar or punctuation errors before you post your work.

If you're not sure whether you are using a word, get help from an online dictionary. Respect your readers as intelligent and well-informed people who could just as easily spend their time elsewhere.

Conclusion

Blogging can be fun, and it can be a good source of income. To blog, you need to commit to posting. Keep your articles simple and easy to read.

You can continue reading our blog to find other tips about how to make money from home.

MAKING MONEY FROM HOME

How to Make Money with Kindle Books and AMS

If you are good at writing and if you can share your knowledge with others, there is a high possibility you can make a decent amount of money with Amazon Kindle Publishing. In fact, you will be able to upload your own book and start making money within just 72 hours.

This is one of the most convenient methods available for you to publish a book and make money. That's because you don't need to go through the hassle of finding a book deal, signing an agreement with an agent and going through the frustrating process with a publisher.

Here are the steps that you will need to follow in order to make money with Kindle Books and AMS.

Keep an eye on the popular authors in your genre

As the first thing, you need to do research and get to know the popular authors who belong to your genre. When you go through one of his/her books, you will be able to see a section called "Customers who bought this item also bought".

This is a section that Amazon is using in order to recommend new books to the readers. If you want to promote your new book on Amazon, this will be one of the best opportunities available.

To increase the chances of making your book appear on this list, you can bid heavily on the books offered by your competitors, so that you will be able to make your book visible on all their book pages.

This way you will be able to steal the show and grab more attention from the users who are interested.

Target the books, which were recently transformed into movies

The books that were recently transformed into movies will be hot releases in Amazon. Due to this reason, you are encouraged to target them as well.

You can look for the movies that are being created under your genre. This way you can see whether there are any Amazon books behind them.

If you can find any books, you can go ahead and target them. This will help you increase the number of sales that you make.

Use Amazon Marketing Services (AMS)

Use AMS to advertise your books. This is one sure way to get your books showing at the top of an Amazon page when people search for a book or a topic.

Advertising on AMS takes a lot of experimentation to get right. However, when done right, can make you lots of money.

Make sure to check out Marco Moutinho's AMS Ads Profit Formula. It's a course that I took, which I can recommend.

All I can say that his course works. With this course, I quickly learned how to create ads on Amazon for my Kindle books that are profitable. Ever since then, my sales have gone up 10 times.

Marco's step-by-step instructions are easy to follow. You will be given access to videos you can pause, rewind or re-watch to understand even more.

Marco will show you how to join Amazon Marketing Services on the US, UK, and Canada. Most importantly, you will learn how to advertise and be profitable. Selling books, making more money and spending less on ads.

You can sign up for the course, which is risk-free, money-back guarantee; you can start applying your knowledge soon. The best part is that you get to ask questions directly to Marco via the Facebook group that accompanies the course.

Use negative keywords on AMS

Using negative keywords to ensure success with AMS is one of the lesser-known secrets, but you can consider it as well. This is not something difficult to do. The results you get out of this method is totally worth when compared to the efforts you spend.

If there is an epic fantasy novel, which is loved by the teens, but hated by the adults, you can think of using negative keywords to enhance the visibility of your books.

You don't need to worry about getting one-star reviews for your book from the unsatisfied audiences. You just need to be concerned about the improved results that you will get at the end of the day.

Use AMS for the reviews

You can think about spending a bit of extra money on AMS throughout a promo that you have scheduled. Then you will be able to get an excellent return out of your investment in the long run.

You will also be amazed at the number of downloads that you will be able to receive at the end of the day.

You need to make sure that you are adding a call for reviews. This should be mentioned at the end of the book. You cannot expect a lot of readers to leave reviews. But you will at least get a few honest reviews out of this method.

Take a look at Advertising Outside Amazon

You should never limit yourself to the advertisements of Amazon Marketing Services. You can think about investing your money on Facebook Ads, BookBub ads, and other advertising methods.

You will not have to invest thousands of dollars on these advertising platforms as well. You will only be spending a small amount of money and it can provide you with amazing results at the end of the day.

Resources

- The AMS Ads Profit Formula course.
- Facebook Ads
- BookBub Ads

Making Money From Home Selling Stock Photography

If you're a regular denizen of the internet, odds are that, at some point, you've come across a stock photography website – Shutterstock, Getty, iStockPhoto, or the like. And after perusing the prices required for most of the big-res pictures, odds are that, after grumbling about them for a little while, you said to yourself "hey, I like to take pictures; I could make a bit of side-cash selling mine on one of these sites, right?"

And you're certainly not wrong–play it right, and you can make money from home at a pretty decent rate. But just like with any market that involves high demand and lots of competition, you need to approach it correctly, or you could potentially end up out of pocket. So just to get you started, here are a few basic tips for selling your snaps to some stock photography site.

Get the Right Equipment

Now that there's a camera on pretty much every smartphone, more and more people are becoming wise to the simple excitement of photography. But most photography sites aren't just going to accept your iPhone selfies–the market would be even more crowded if they did.

No, to sell stock photos, you're first going to need to equip yourself with a high-quality camera. Precisely how good you'll need it to be varies; but in general, most photography sites require photos to be, at the least, about 4 megapixels each. Swing for something that can shoot at least several notches above that.

And if possible, consider also getting some extras – tripods and the like. The better quality of your pictures, the higher the chance of the site accepting them, and of people buying them.

Take the Right Pictures

If you're still not sure exactly *what* you'd like to take pictures, you'd do well to check out the latest stock photography trends.

Like most things on the internet, stock photography is heavily influenced by the latest trends and crazes. Over the course of 2018, some noted trends included minimalist compositions and pastel colours (the two of which frequently overlapped), as well as social themes, such as cultural diversity and challenging gender roles.

Pop onto the internet's bigger stock photography sites, and check out what sort of pictures are currently getting the most views, in order to get an idea of what sort of things are big at the moment.

On the other hand, if you do have a certain subject matter that you'd like to focus on in your photography, that's perfectly fine as well. But do consider going onto those sites anyway and checking out on which of them that particular subject matter seems to do best.

Sell On the Right Platform

There are, as you're probably well aware, countless sites out there dedicated to selling stock photography; but you'd do best not to pick the one that just pops up first on Google. Instead, peruse their terms of service and requirements. Consider whether the photographs you take will meet their standards, whether they get enough traffic, what sort of prices the pictures on there usually sell for, and what sort of cut of those sales the site takes. If possible, seek out professional photographers who have sold stock photos in the past, and try to get some recommendations from them.

And of course, if you feel confident enough, you could always take the approach of purchasing your own online domain, and selling your photos through that. It's a bit more risky, and you'll have to do even more marketing; but on the other hand, you won't have a bigger site taking a cut off your sales.

MAKING MONEY FROM HOME – PART 2

How to Make Money with Kindle Books

If you are good at writing and if you can share your knowledge with others, there is a high possibility for you to make a decent amount of money with Amazon Kindle Publishing. In fact, you will be able to have your own book and start making money within just 72 hours.

This is one of the most convenient methods available for you to publish a book and make money. That's because you don't need to go through the hassle of finding a book deal, signing an agreement with an agent and going through the frustrating process with a publisher. Here are the steps that you will need to follow in order to make money with Kindle Books and AMS.

- Keep an eye on the popular authors in your genre

As the first thing, you need to do a research and get to know about the popular authors who belong to your genre. When you go through one of his/her books, you will be able to see a section called "Customers who bought this item also bought". This is a section that Amazon is using in order to recommend new books to the readers. If you want to promote your new book on Amazon, this will be one of the best opportunities available.

To increase the chances of making your book appear on this list, you can bid heavily on the books offered by your competitors, while targeting, so that you will be able to make your book visible on all their book pages. Then you will be able to steal the show and grab more attention from the users who are interested.

- Focus on the books that are published by Amazon

Next, you can focus on the books that are published by Amazon. Amazon has got many imprints, which they use in order to publish books. Thomas and Mercer is the most prominent one out of them. Targeting the books and authors who come from these subsidiary companies can be considered as a great idea.

The Amazon algorithm prefers to make other people purchase stuff from them. You need to try your best in order to get your books closer to the Amazon babies. Then you will be happy with the results that you are getting in the long run.

- Target the books, which were recently transformed into movies

The books that were recently transformed into movies will be hot releases in Amazon. Due to this reason, you are encouraged to target them as well. You can look for the movies that are being created under your genre. Then you can see whether there are any Amazon books behind them. If you can find any books, you can go ahead and target them. This will help you to increase the number of sales that you make.

- Use negative keywords

Using negative keywords to ensure success with AMS is one of the lesser-known secrets, but you can consider it as well. This is not something difficult to do. The results you get out of this method is totally worth when compared to the efforts you spend.

If there is an epic fantasy novel, which is loved by the teens, but hated by the adults, you can think of using negative keywords to enhance the visibility of your books. You don't need to worry about getting one star reviews for your book from the unsatisfied audiences. You just need to be concerned about the improved results that you are getting at the end of the day.

- Use AMS for the reviews

You can think about spending a bit of extra money on AMS throughout a promo that you have scheduled. Then you will be able to get an excellent return out of your investment in the long run. You will also be amazed with the number of downloads that you will be able to receive at the end of the day.

You need to make sure that you are adding a call for reviews. This should be mentioned at the end of the book. You cannot expect a lot of readers to leave reviews. But you will at least get few honest reviews out of this method.

- Pre-populate your book with pre-orders

This is another investment opportunity available for you to consider. You can think about pre-populating your book on Amazon with pre-orders. If you can do targeting in the right way, you will be able to add your book into the "Customers who bought this item also bought" section as well. Therefore, you will be able to get a recommendation loop from Amazon.

You can pre-populate your book with pre-orders, before one week or several months in advance. If your author platform is a bigger one, there is a possibility for you to pre-populate the book well in advance of the real publication date. You shouldn't be too worried about the amount that you spend on this. That's because it can provide you with some amazing results at the end of the day.

You can think about investing your money on Facebook Ads, BookBub ads, and other advertising methods. You will not have to invest thousands of dollars on these advertising platforms as well. You will only be spending a small amount of money and it can provide you with amazing results at the end of the day.

KINDLE MONEY MASTERY REVIEW

Have you ever wanted to make a passive income from the Internet apart from your traditional job? Then Kindle Money Mastery is something that you need to consider about. The main objective of Kindle Money Mastery is to teach you how to make money online by selling eBooks. With the development of technology, the demand and popularity of eBooks are increasing and you can think of this method without any hesitation.

What is Kindle Money Mastery?

Kindle Money Mastery is an electronic product, but it differs a lot from the other similar products that you can find on the Internet. Stefan Pylarinos is the creator of this program, who has made millions of dollars through publishing eBooks on Amazon Kindle. He has shared his success story and the tricks that he used to reach success through Kindle Money Mastery.

This step-by-step training program will taking you the entire process of making money out of eBook publishing in Amazon. You just need to follow the instructions and become an expert in eBook publishing. For example, it will let you know how to create content and what is the process that you need to follow when publishing them.

Who can try Kindle Money Mastery?

You don't need to possess any publishing or technical skills to follow Kindle Money Mastery. The training program is strong enough to make anyone an eBook publisher. It will even let you know how to choose the most profitable niches, how to create a title for your eBook, how to do a proper keyword research and how to get rid of frustration that is associated through the entire process.

The Kindle Money Mastery membership program has more than 20 video tutorial lessons to make the life easy for you. Apart from that, you can find four bonus videos that explain the secrets of eBook publishing. You can also get access to over 4 templates and 20 PDF downloads that can be used to get some assistance in eBook publishing.

Keyword research

Before you start selling your books on Amazon Kindle, it is important for you to do an appropriate keyword research. This can contribute a lot towards the positive results that you will get. Kindle Money Mastery will be able to help you with that.

A series of videos are presented to you through Kindle Money Mastery, which will help you learn how to find the appropriate keywords according to your niche. Then you will be able to use those keywords and make sure that your books become popular ones in the niche. You will be able to learn some lesser known secrets about keyword research by this program as well.

Book titles

The book titles that you use for your books on Amazon Kindle can also provide you with outstanding results. Therefore, you should be careful to use appropriate book titles. Kindle Money Mastery can help you to figure out those book titles.

In fact, Kindle Money Mastery will teach you the criteria, which you need to follow in order to create the book titles as well as subtitles. These titles will be in a position to capture the attention of readers. Therefore, you will be able to get outstanding results at the end of the day.

Book covers

The covers that you use for the books on Amazon can also provide you with outstanding results. Therefore, you should be careful to use appropriate book covers. Kindle Money Mastery can provide a great help to you with that as well.

Kindle Money Mastery can teach you the marketplaces that you can access in order to hire a book cover designer according to your preferences. By following these steps, you will be able to hire a book cover designer by spending minimum efforts. In addition, you can make sure that you will be able to get the book cover designed with a minimum investment as well.

Book creation

The steps that you follow when creating the book can provide you with outstanding assistance when you sell it. Kindle Money Mastery will let you know about those book cover creation secrets as well. Therefore, you can easily understand how to make a decent quality book. However, you need to keep in mind that Kindle Money Mastery is not a book publishing course. It will only provide you with guidance on how to create an effective book.

Marketing

Last but not least, Kindle Money Mastery will teach you how to take your Amazon book publishing efforts to the next level with marketing techniques. You can learn multiple methods, which can help you with marketing your book. You will also be able to learn how to market your book outside Amazon. The marketing techniques offered to you with Kindle Money Mastery are up to date and you will always be able to end up with positive results by following them.

Access to private Facebook group

All the people who purchase Kindle Money Mastery can get access to a Facebook group that is filled with Amazon Kindle eBook publishers. You can post all your concerns in the group and the others will answer them within few minutes. In addition, you can go through the posts shared by them and enhance your knowledge on eBook publishing. The entire program is focused on how to make money with Kindle publishing.

Conclusion

If you assume that Amazon Kindle Money Mastery is something available for the people who can write well, you are wrong. It will let you know how to write top selling content under a profitable niche and how to make money within a short time. It has covered everything that you need to know about Kindle eBooks. Therefore, any person who has an interest in making money through the Internet can spend their money to purchase Kindle Money Mastery.

Find Profitable Keywords For Your Kindle Books

You are investing a considerable amount of time and money to write a book and publish it on Amazon. After you publish a book by spending such a lot of efforts, you expect people to go ahead and spend their money in purchasing the book.

Unfortunately, most of the self-published books on Amazon fail to achieve the targeted amount of sales in a timely manner. In fact, around 250 copies are being sold in an average self-published book for a lifetime. But you don't need to worry about anything. That's because there are some effective methods, which you can follow in order to increase the number of sales that you will be able to make by selling your books on Amazon. That's where you can take a look at KDP Rocket.

What is KDP Rocket?

KDP Rocket can simply be defined as a keyword research tool. It is also possible for you to consider this as a market research tool. You will be able to use this tool in Amazon marketplace to determine whether a specific books is feasible or not. This tool can help you to do such extensive research on both fiction and non-fiction books on Amazon.

When you get your hands on KDP Rocket, you don't need to depend on intuition or guesswork. It will provide you with all the relevant information, which you can use in order to make decisions without any hassle. Therefore, even a person who is publishing a book on Amazon for the very first time will be able to end up with positive and measurable results, without any hassle.

What can you learn with KDP Rocket?

You may have excellent writing skills. But if you cannot offer what the readers are searching for, it will not be possible for you to get any measurable results out of the writing skills that you have. That's where you can think about getting your hands on KDP Rocket. Writing blindly without any validation of the market will just make you waste your time. Therefore, you should have a clear understanding on how to write a book correctly and overcome the negative consequences linked with selling it.

When you are following KDP Rocket, you will be able to understand what types of books that people are searching for. Then you will be able to align your books accordingly to make them cater the needs of people. KDP Rocket can provide you with real time stats as well. You can easily figure out the number of individuals who are looking for the books that belong to your niche every single month. On the other hand, you can understand the amount of money that authors who belong to that niche will be able to earn.

Can KDP Rocket help you to end up with positive results?

Before you spend your money on KDP Rocket, you will wonder whether it is in a position to provide you with any positive results or not. Yes, KDP Rocket can provide you with positive results and you don't need to worry about anything. The information that you will be able to get out of the book can help you in many ways.

First of all, you will need to understand the things that you should do to your book in order to make it a top selling product in the marketplace. There are easy methods of making your book a top selling product. You can understand those secrets by following this program. On the other hand, you can also understand whether writing a book under the genre that you have in your mind is worth it or not. When you gather all essential information from [KDP Rocket](), you will be able to proceed and write your book. This can provide you with outstanding results and you can make sure that you are not spending your money in vain.

How much does it cost to get KDP Rocket?

To purchase [KDP Rocket](), you will have to spend $97. If you are an author on Amazon, or if you are willing to generate a passive income by selling books on Amazon, this is an opportunity that you shouldn't ignore. You will be able to cover up your investment within a short period of time.

You should also keep in mind that the fee of $97 is inclusive, and it doesn't contain any hidden charges. This can also help you to keep peace of mind when you purchase the book. You can make sure that you are getting what you want for the amount that you spend and you will not have to spend any additional amounts of money for the book in the long run.

Why should you get KDP Rocket?

A variety of online money-making opportunities are available for the people in today's world. Out of those opportunities, [KDP Rocket]() will provide you with one of the best opportunities. You will be able to earn a decent amount of money with the knowledge and guidance that you will be able to get out of this program.

If you are an existing author on Amazon or if you are planning to become an author in Amazon, you can get your hands on KDP Rocket. It will never disappoint you and it will provide you with the results that you want. This guide provides you with all the essential information that you need to know from the basics. They include coming up with titles to your book, creating the subtitles of the book and even writing the book description as well.

Conclusion

As you can see, KDP Rocket is a great guide available for any person to boost the number of sales that can be made by selling books on Amazon. You can go ahead and try out this program without keeping any doubts or second thoughts in your mind. It can provide you with measurable and outstanding results.

Increase Sales of Your Kindle Books

Are you looking for a convenient and a hassle free method to boost your Amazon sales? Then The AMS Ads Profit Formula is one of the best methods available out there to consider. Any person who is just starting to sell on Amazon or even the experienced Amazon sellers out there can think about getting their hands on The AMS Ads Profit Formula.

What is The AMS Ads Profit Formula?

The AMS Ads Profit Formula can simply be defined as a guide, which can assist you to increase the sales that you will make on Amazon with selling books. You don't need to have previous experience with selling books on Amazon to get started with this. You can start off with a minimum knowledge and you will be able to learn all the basics. Then you will be able to follow the techniques and end up with amazing results.

Who is the author behind The AMS Ads Profit Formula?

Marcos Mouthino is the author behind The AMS Ads Profit Formula. He was a hustler in the past who was struggling hard to build up an extra income. He was taking a look at multiple sources of passive income. After a lot of research, he figured out that publishing books on Amazon can help him to receive outstanding results. The knowledge that he used to make such a passive income is shared through The AMS Ads Profit Formula.

Who should purchase The AMS Ads Profit Formula?

The AMS Ads Profit Formula is the ultimate guide, which the Amazon booksellers should purchase. If you are about to start selling books on Amazon or if you are struggling to make more sales for the books that you sell on Amazon, you can think about getting your hands on The AMS Ads Profit Formula.

No matter to what genre the books that you sell on Amazon belong to, you will be able to get outstanding results out of The AMS Ads Profit Formula. You just need to follow what is being mentioned in this guide and you will be able to end up with amazing results. In fact, you will see measurable results in the sale of your books along with time.

What can you learn with The AMS Ads Profit Formula?

You will be able to learn a lot about increasing the sales that you make on Amazon with the assistance of this guide. Leveraging the power of advertisements hold a prominent place out of them. They include everything from the basics, including ad creation. For example, you can learn how to create appropriate advertisements, and how to add the keywords.

The AMS Ads Profit Formula will also teach you how much money you should be spending on your advertisements on a daily basis. It will show you that you don't need to spend a lot of money on expensive advertising campaigns to end up with positive results. You just need to spend a minimum on the advertising campaigns and you will be able to witness positive results within a short period of time.

Is The AMS Ads Profit Formula worth the price?

The AMS Ads Profit Formula is not a guide that comes for free. You will have to spend a considerable amount of money out of your pocket to purchase this guide. However, it will not take a lot of time to recover your investment. That's because the content written in The AMS Ads Profit Formula is highly effective and you will be able to follow it and end up with positive results. In other words, you will be able to receive high profits with your book selling efforts on Amazon.

The ability of The AMS Ads Profit Formula to deliver positive results has been proven. The customer reviews available about this guide on the internet bear testimonials to prove the above-mentioned fact. As per the customer reviews, you will be able to cover up the investment within just two months of purchasing the book. Therefore, you don't need to keep any doubts in your mind when you go ahead and buy it. It can provide you with outstanding results.

Pros of The AMS Ads Profit Formula

- The AMS Ads Profit Formula is a straightforward guide that you can follow. You will never get confused with the content presented by it. You can simply go through the facts and understand what is written. Then you can apply them to your bookselling efforts on Amazon to increase the sales volume.
- Marco has done a perfect job by organizing this course. You will be able to learn everything from the basics as a result of it. In other words, you can see the basic lessons at the beginning of the course and things will get advance along with time.
- When you purchase The AMS Ads Profit Formula, you will be able to get many documents. These documents provide invaluable resources to the sellers on Amazon. They can transform the way how you are using the power of ads to improve the bookselling efforts in Amazon.

- When you purchase The AMS Ads Profit Formula you can make sure that you are not spending your money on fluff. Marco has only provided you with the content that you need to know in order to end up with success.

Cons of The AMS Ads Profit Formula

- In some lessons, Marco goes straight into the content. He doesn't provide any background information about it. It's better if he had included some background information as well.
- This is available only on digital format.

Conclusion

If you are looking forward to generate a passive income, selling books on Amazon is a great opportunity that you can consider. But before you do that, you need to be aware of how to generate more sales. Otherwise, you will get fed up and give it up. When you are following The AMS Ads Profit Formula, you can make sure that you don't end up with such consequences.

Make Money with Affiliate Marketing

Among the methods available out there for the people to make a passive income, affiliate marketing has received a lot of attention. It is a quick and a straightforward method available for the interested individuals to make a decent income at the comfort of home. But before you start making money with affiliate marketing, you should have a clear understanding of what it is and what you need to do in order to make money with it.

What exactly is affiliate marketing?

Affiliate marketing is one of the oldest marketing practices. In here, you will be marketing the product or service that another party offers. All you have to do is to find the buyers for the products and services. If you are successful with your marketing efforts and if you can make a buyer purchase a product or a service, you will be able to receive a percentage of the commission. This marketing method is simple as that and it can provide you with outstanding results in the long run.

How to get started with affiliate marketing?

Individuals who are about to start affiliate marketing have a variety of options available to consider. You can go through these available options and get started with the perfect options out of them. Among the available options, Amazon affiliate holds a prominent place. In here, you will need to promote the products and services that are available on Amazon. If you are successful with selling them, you will be able to earn a commission from Amazon.

A variety of methods are available for you to promote the products as well. Creating a website or a blog holds a prominent place out of them. You can review the products or services in the website or blog that you create. Then you will be able to insert your affiliate link into the same post as well. When people go through the content and feel like buying the product or the service, they will go through your affiliate link. As a result, you will be able to end up making a commission.

Be patient with affiliate marketing

Even though affiliate marketing is one of the best methods available for you to make money online, you cannot get rich overnight with it. It is important for you to be patient when you engage with affiliate marketing and it can provide you with outstanding results. For example, if you are building a website to help your affiliate marketing efforts, you need to find products to promote and then you need to feed content. You should then focus on promoting your website or blog among potential audiences.

Select attractive products

The products that you select for affiliate marketing are in a position to contribute a lot towards the number of sales that you will be able to make at the end of the day. Therefore, you should be careful to select attractive products as much as possible. If there is a high demand for the product or service that you promote, you will be able to get people buy it through your affiliate link without any hassle.

Finding such attractive products is not an easy thing to do. You will need to conduct research in the market and figure out the demand that is available for them. Investing your time and money on this effort is totally worth when compared to the benefits that you will be able to get in the long run. Therefore, you can think about following it without keeping any doubts or second thoughts in your mind.

Use multiple sources of traffic

If you can drive more traffic towards your affiliate blog or website, you will be able to make more sales with it. However, this is one of the biggest challenges that you should overcome. You should never seek the assistance of bots in order to drive more traffic towards your website or blog. You need to focus only on organic traffic, as the bots are not in a position to provide you with effective results.

To get better results, you can focus on multiple sources of traffic. Google AdWords is one perfect source out of them. Then you can think about promoting your website or blog on social media networks as well. Then you will be able to see more people coming towards your blog, which can increase the number of sales that are being made through your affiliate links. This can contribute towards your success at the end of the day.

Try to attract targeted traffic

Some people tend to promote their affiliate blogs and websites in irrelevant places. Doing this will not be able to provide you with any positive results. Instead, you need to think about promoting your blog or website among people who are interested in purchasing the products or services that you promote. You can also do a research to figure that out.

Article marketing is a good method available for you to go ahead with. This can help you to boost your search engine rankings. Therefore, you can drive more targeted traffic towards your website. Then you can think about email marketing. Email marketing is not dead, and it is still in a position to provide affiliate marketers with amazing results. You just need to focus on finding the appropriate mailing lists and promoting the products or services with them.

Conclusion

As you can see, affiliate marketing is a great method that you can follow in order to make money online. You don't need to have your own products or services to make money with affiliate marketing. All you have to do is to promote the products or services that other parties offer. Then you will be able to make money for every sale that you make.

Make Money With The Super Affiliate System

A variety of effective programs are available for the affiliate marketers to purchase and ensure their success in the future. The Super Affiliate System holds a prominent place out of them. If you are struggling for your success as an affiliate marketer, look no further as this is one of the biggest opportunities available for you to consider.

What is The Super Affiliate System?

The Super Affiliate System can be considered as a program, which has the ability to help you drive a massive volume of traffic towards the products and services that you promote through your affiliate marketing efforts. With this much of traffic, you will be able to earn a six figure or a seven figure income with ease. The best thing about The Super Affiliate System is that you will be able to get multiple daily commissions with the traffic that you get.

You don't need to worry about the products that you promote and the way how you promote them. The traffic outranks them all. Therefore, any affiliate marketer will be able to earn a significant income through the affiliate marketing efforts by following this program. You will be impressed with the results that it can provide to you in the long run.

What can you get with The Super Affiliate System?

Before you get your hands on The Super Affiliate System, you need to have a clear understanding of what it offers. Then you can determine whether the amount you spend to get your hands on The Super Affiliate System is worth it or not. With The Super Affiliate System, you will be able to get a comprehensive six week training on how to become a paid affiliate marketer. In addition to that, you will be able to get access to a comprehensive video training course of over 60 hours.

All the videos that you can find in The Super Affiliate System are created by the author of the program. Therefore, you don't need to keep any doubts in mind about the reliability of content that you will get. You can always ensure that you are ending up with the best possible results by following content available in The Super Affiliate System.

What kind of training can you get with The Super Affiliate System?

With The Super Affiliate System, you will be able to get a comprehensive training on how to boost your affiliate marketing efforts with traffic generation. You will be able to understand how to leverage multiple platforms and drive traffic towards your affiliate links. In other words, you can understand the different methods available for you to improve the overall visibility of your affiliate links.

The training The Super Affiliate System provides to you can help you to understand Google AdWords and Facebook Ads. These sources can provide a lot of traffic to you. You can figure out the secrets to boost traffic through the program and you will be able to get outstanding results. In addition to that, The Super Affiliate

System will also teach you how to boost traffic with YouTube ads and native ads.

Who can follow this program?

The content available through The Super Affiliate System is written in simplest form. Therefore, even a person who doesn't have previous experience with affiliate marketing will be able to follow it. On the other hand, the experienced affiliate marketers, who are looking forward to boost their traffic to affiliate links and increase the commission amount will be able to follow The Super Affiliate System. You just need to invest six weeks on this program and it will then provide you with outstanding results that you will love.

Should I wait for six weeks to get results?

Yes, if you are following The Super Affiliate System, you will need to wait for a period of six weeks to get positive results. It will not be possible for you to apply the knowledge that you gain straightaway. You must learn all the background information and apply them accordingly to get positive results. The program is designed in a way to make you accountable as a student. Hence, it is important for you to stay committed to the program for the duration of six weeks. Then you will be provided with the freedom to go ahead and make money as much as you want with improved freedom.

What else can you get with The Super Affiliate System?

Now you have a basic understanding about the core content that you will be able to get with The Super Affiliate System. While keeping that in your mind, you can take a look at the other tools that you can get along with this program. They include:

- Landing pages
- Affiliate advertisements to use.
- Access to a private Facebook group, which you can use to interact with the author and like-minded affiliate marketers.
- Weekly coaching sessions.
- Top affiliate marketing efforts that you can use.

What other things should you keep in mind when you purchase The Super Affiliate System?

Before you purchase The Super Affiliate System, you should also keep in mind that the program is backed up with a 30 day money-back guarantee. If you don't receive any positive results within 30 days, you can simply get back the amount that you spent. This clearly shows that the author is extremely serious about the product and he guarantees that all people who use it can end up with receiving positive results at the end of the day.

Conclusion

Among the affiliate marketer training guides available for you to consider, The Super Affiliate System has received a lot of attention. If you are looking for success with your affiliate marketing efforts, you can go ahead and try out The The Super Affiliate System without keeping any doubts in mind. All you have to do is to stay committed for the duration of six weeks where you learn the facts. Then you can apply your knowledge and earn a six figure income with affiliate marketing.

MAKING MONEY FROM HOME

MAKING MONEY FROM HOME

The Freelance Profit Academy Review

Are you good with writing? Do you want to quit your job and start working as a writer? Then you must take a look at the opportunities offered to you by The Freelance Profit Academy. It can be considered as one of the most impressive guides available for the individuals to purchase and learn how to take their freelancing efforts to the next level as writers.

What is The Freelance Profit Academy?

The Freelance Profit Academy can be considered as a comprehensive guide, which is designed for the use of individuals, who are looking forward to become freelance writers in the future. You just need to have the ambition to become a freelance writer and The Freelance Profit Academy will teach you how to achieve it. In fact, The Freelance Profit Academy can let you know how you will be able to earn a six figure income by just working as a freelance writer.

You just need to invest 8 weeks of your time to receive the positive results that The Freelance Profit Academy will offer. At the end of 8th week, you will be aware of some of the best-kept secrets and tools that people can use in order to work as freelance content writers and make a decent amount of money at the comfort of home. You don't need to spend anything out of your pocket to become a freelance content writer. The Freelance Profit Academy will teach you a free method, which you can follow and end up with amazing results at the end of the day.

The success launchpad

The success launchpad is the very first module that you can find in The Freelance Profit Academy. It will provide you with an introduction to freelance content writing. You can understand 5 different methods that you can follow in order to make money as a freelance content writer. In addition, you will be able to figure out how to approach businesses as a freelance content writer. You will also be introduced to few mindset hacks, which can help you to remain focused and get your work done.

Make your efforts visible

When you are working as a freelance content writer, it is important for you to make your efforts visible. Then you will be able to get more work to you. The second module clearly explains the steps, which you need to follow in order to make your efforts visible. For example, The Freelance Profit Academy will teach you how to create a website and promote your freelance content writing services.

Attracting clients

The third module of The Freelance Profit Academy explains how to attract clients. They will not just be ordinary clients. Instead, you will be able to attract better clients, who are willing to pay bigger paycheck to you. In addition, you will be able to figure out how to get better testimonials and many referrals to help you make your life easy with finding clients in the future.

Working with clients

On the fourth module of The Freelance Profit Academy, you will be provided with information on how to work along with clients. You will also be provided with knowledge on how to stay away from the scams, which will take place. Most importantly, this section will introduce you to few automation tools, which you can use in order to automate your Craigslist job searches.

Tripling your income

When you are working as a freelance content writer, you will come across the requirement to increase your income along with time. There are few secret techniques, which you will be able to follow in order to increase your income in a convenient manner. The Freelance Profit Academy will let you know about those secrets as well. You will be introduced to those techniques in a step-by-step manner. Hence, you will never come across any difficulties when you are trying to understand the content. At the end of the week, you will be aware of the steps, which you should follow in order to make a six figure income by working as a freelance content writer.

Autopilot clients

While working as a freelance content writer, you will have a limited amount of time to get your work done. That's where you need to think about automating some activities. Then you can ensure that you don't have to spend any manual efforts to get work done. The Freelance Profit Academy can let you know how to autopilot your clients. Then you will be able to let clients find your services and you don't need to spend any time or efforts on finding clients manually.

How to keep higher paying clients

If you can keep the higher paying clients, you will be able to make sure that you reach all your financial goals with minimum efforts. The Freelance Profit Academy will share some useful and effective secrets, which you can follow in order to retain your highest paying clients. Therefore, you can make sure that you are spending minimum efforts to get more results at the end of the day.

Quitting your day job

It is not worth to follow your day time job because you can invest that time on working as a freelance content writer and make more money. However, most of the individuals tend to think twice before quitting the day time jobs. The Freelance Profit Academy will help you to change your mindset. Therefore, you will be able to quit your day time job without any hassle and make sure that you stick to your career as a freelance content writer to achieve financial freedom.

Conclusion

As you can see, The Freelance Profit Academy is the best product that freelance content writers can purchase. Even if you are looking forward to become a freelance content writer in the future, you can follow The Freelance Profit Academy and make sure that you get the best possible results at the end of the day.

MAKE MONEY WITH CLICKBANK

ClickBank is one of the best platforms available for the affiliate marketers and vendors to use. If you are a person who is planning to get into affiliate marketing, you can take a look at ClickBank without keeping any doubts in mind. However, it is better if you can get to know about ClickBank, before you sign up with it and start making money. That's where CB University will be able to assist you with.

What is CB University?

CB University can be considered as a solid course, which will provide you with the understanding on how to create your own digital products and start making money. On the other hand, individuals who work as affiliate marketers will also be able to refer CB University and figure out how they will be able to take their affiliate marketing efforts to the next level. The content available in CB University is up to date and you will be able to follow it and end up with extremely positive results.

8-week training for the affiliate marketers

Affiliate marketers who take a look at CB University will be able to get their hands on a 8-week training program. You don't need to have any previous experience with affiliate marketing in order to follow this training program. You will be able to learn everything from the scratch and determine the secrets behind promoting digital products to make high commissions at the end of the day.

12-week training for the vendors

CB University is a guide that vendors can follow as well. You will be introduced to a comprehensive 12-week training program, which the vendors will be able to follow. This is an informative training program. The training program can help you to create your own digital products and then start selling them online to make profits.

CB University will help you to brainstorm and research what the best niche available for you to go ahead with. Then you will be able to figure out how to create your own digital products from the scratch and create a sales funnel for it. In addition to that, you will also be able to figure out how to drive traffic towards the landing page. When you follow the steps as mentioned in CB University, you will be able to make sure that you get a decent income by selling the digital products that you create on ClickBank.

Weekly Q&A Webinar

All people who purchase CB University will be able to gain access to a weekly Q&A webinar as well. On this webinar, it is possible to ask questions from Adam and Justin directly. Therefore, you can make sure that you don't anything without any knowledge. You can always get your work done in an effective manner and overcome hassle or frustration.

However, you need to keep in mind that these weekly webinars are not based upon specific topics. They will be filled with random questions and answers. However, you will be able to get a lot of questions answered with the assistance of these webinars. Hence, you will be able to refrain from making mistakes.

Access to private Facebook group

When you purchase CB University, you will also be able to gain access to a Facebook support group. This Facebook support group is filled with like-minded individuals. Therefore, you will be able to get an excellent support and assistance for the issues that you are dealing with. The activeness and level of engagement that can be found in the Facebook group would impress you. Therefore, you will be able to learn a lot of new things and stay up to date with the trends by being a member of this Facebook Group.

Access to ClickBank Builder

Along with the purchase of CB University, you will be able to gain access to many upselling tools as well. The ClickBank builder holds a prominent place out of them. This is one of the most useful tools, which can assist you to develop professional looking websites with ease. In addition to websites, this tool will also let you know the steps that you must follow in order to create offer pages and landing pages.

You don't need to have any technical knowledge to use ClickBank builder and get your work done. Instead, you can use the convenient drag-and-drop features to make the life easy for you. Therefore, you will appreciate this tool, which you will be able to get exclusively with CB University.

CBU Toolkit

CBU Toolkit can also be considered as another upsell tool that you can get along with CB University. This is another impressive tool that you can get. It will provide you with access to many other tools, which can be used to run an online business successfully. For example, CB University Toolkit will provide you with social media tools, email service provider and a website domain finder.

Is CB University a scam?

Now you must be wondering whether CB University is a scam, or it is in a position to provide you with outstanding results. This product is not a scam. That's because you will be able to get the training you need from the legit training resources and real coaches. They will provide up-to-date information on how to make money through ClickBank. Therefore, you don't need to keep any second thoughts in mind while you are spending money out of your pocket to gain access to CB University.

Conclusion

Creating digital products and affiliate marketing are in a position to help a person make a living online. If you want to experience such financial freedom, all you have to do is to take a look at CB University. It will provide you with the knowledge that you need to take your online money-making efforts to the next level.

Learn How To Generate Traffic To Your Website

Traffic and leads play a major role behind the success of online businesses that exist out there in the world. Therefore, it is important for you to get your hands on the appropriate sources of traffic. In addition, you need to think about boosting the volume of traffic that your online business is receiving. Then you will not have to worry too much about the sales volume that you make. It can even keep you away from expensive marketing campaigns. That's where Traffic Multiplier will be able to assist you with.

What is Traffic Multiplier?

Traffic Multiplier can be considered as a proven and an effective traffic generation software. It comes along with a comprehensive training package as well. The video training can help you to understand how to generate more traffic and leads into your online business. Therefore, you can easily understand how to increase your customer base, along with the sales volume that you make.

Traffic Multiplier can also show you a detailed technique, which you can follow in order to generate sales along with target audiences. Therefore, you will be able to cover up the amount that you spend to get your hands on Traffic Multiplier within a short period of time. You will appreciate the results that this program can provide to you in the long run as well.

Comprehensive training course

Traffic Multiplier provides you with access to a comprehensive training course on how to get more traffic towards your online business. You don't need to have any previous experience or knowledge with traffic generation to understand the content. You will be able to follow the training videos and figure out all important information on how to generate traffic. In addition, you will be able to understand how to ensure ongoing profits with the traffic that you can generate.

Creating two different lists in one

Another innovative feature that you can discover in Traffic Multiplier is that it helps you to create two different lists in one. In other words, it can help you to get both push notification leads and email subscribers. Therefore, you will be able to quickly connect with the audiences. You will be provided with multiple methods to connect with the audiences and multiply the profits you will be earning at the end of the day.

Instant monetization

You would not want to wait for a long period of time to receive profits from the new leads that you make. Instead, you would prefer to gain instant profits from the leads that you find. Traffic Multiplier will be able to provide an excellent assistance to you with that as well. You will be able to gain profits from the leads as soon as they subscribe. Therefore, you don't need to worry about the effectiveness of the training program.

Guaranteed return on investment

You don't need to keep any doubts or second thoughts in your mind with this investment opportunity. That's because it guarantees the return that you will be able to get out of your investment. The other similar programs like this will leak traffic. It will cost you with more amounts of money.

However, Traffic Multiplier will come along with unique techniques, which you will be able to follow in order to figure out how to follow up with the visitors that do not get converted on the very first attempt. You will also be able to understand how to generate more and more subscribers on the list, without spending a fortune.

Endless scaling opportunities

Traffic Multiplier will expose you to endless scaling opportunities. When you set up everything to generate profits, you will be able to scale with minimum hassle. Therefore, you will be able to get your hands on paid advertisements for generating multiple profits as much as you want.

Automated profits

Out of all features that you can find in Traffic Multiplier, the ability to automate profits is the most outstanding feature. As a person who is trying to make money online, that is your expectation as well. You don't always want to stay in front of the computer to make profits. Instead, you want to automate the flow. Traffic Multiplier will teach you how to do it.

Traffic Multiplier will teach you about the steps, which you need to follow in order to run your campaigns in complete autopilot mode. Therefore, you will be able to generate high-converting and fresh leads at all times. It will also help you to bring in more and more commissions without a lot of effort.

Who should use Traffic Multiplier?

All the individuals who have their online businesses must think about using Traffic Multiplier. This program has specifically been created to provide them with outstanding results. Whether you are an e-commerce marketer, video marketer, affiliate marketer, or a beginner, you will be able to follow Traffic Multiplier and receive positive results. This will help you to take your online businesses to the next level as well.

Traffic Multiplier is extremely easy to use. You don't need to have any special skills or capabilities to use Traffic Multiplier and get the most out of it. On the other hand, it will expose you to a detailed training program. This detailed training program will not leave any doubts in your mind. You will be able to understand the facts and work accordingly to ensure your success in the long run.

Conclusion

Boosting the traffic that you receive to your online store can be considered as the best method that you can follow to make more sales and increase your profits. In order to do that, you can go ahead and take a look at Traffic Multiplier. It will provide you with outstanding results and you will not have to worry about anything. You will be amazed with the results that Traffic Multiplier will be able to provide to you as well.

MAKING MONEY FROM HOME

MAKE MONEY FROM YOUTUBE

YouTube is the most popular video streaming website on the internet. On the other hand, it can be considered as the second most popular search engine in the internet as well. It also provides people with many money-making opportunities as well.

Creating your YouTube channel

Before you start making money from YouTube, you need to understand that the process of making money in YouTube is not something that you can follow to get rich overnight. You will need to go through a series of steps to make your very first dollar. From that point onwards, you will be able to make money with ease.

Uploading content to YouTube

To make money on YouTube, you should first create your YouTube channel. You need to be the owner of the YouTube channel and it will help you to make more money. Then you can add content to the YouTube channel. When adding content, you need to understand that the quality of content can contribute a lot towards the amount of money that you will be able to earn at the end of the day. Therefore, you need to make your videos interesting enough.

Building an audience

After you upload videos, you must think about building an audience for the videos uploaded on YouTube. This is one of the key factors, which can contribute towards the amount of money that you will be able to earn with YouTube. You can keep on uploading interesting content and it will help you to build up a better audience. Your primary objective should be to get more subscribers as much as possible. They will directly help you to increase the total amount of money that you will be able to make.

As the next step, you can think about monetizing the videos on YouTube. If you don't enable monetization on your videos, it will not be possible for you to make money. In fact, allowing monetization can help you to place advertisements on top of your videos.

YouTube AdSense

With this step, you can create YouTube AdSense as well. YouTube AdSense is a part of Google AdSense. You can simply sign up with Google AdSense. However, you need to be at least 18 years old to create a YouTube AdSense account. Then YouTube AdSense advertisements will be displayed on top of your videos.

When the viewers click on those advertisements, you will be able to make money. However, it is important to keep in mind that you cannot earn a significant amount of money by a click. However, it will add up over time and you will be able to make a considerable amount of money. That's why it is important for you to focus more on building an audience. If you have a bigger audience, you don't need to worry too much about the amount that you can make.

Introducing UtubeCash

If you try to make an income with YouTube in the convention way, you will have to invest a considerable amount of time and effort. However, there are some effective shortcuts, which can provide you with outstanding results. You are encouraged to take a look at them, so that you will be able to make more money on YouTube without spending a lot of effort.

UtubeCash can be considered as a perfect example for such a shortcut method that you can follow. UtubeCash is a program that can assist any person to generate a regular income with the assistance of YouTube. You will be able to earn money directly from YouTube and there are no other sources involved with it.

Is UtubeCash for experienced YouTubers?

No, you don't need to be an experienced YouTuber to follow UtubeCash and receive the positive results that are delivered by it. Any person will be able to follow the steps and understand how to make a decent amount of money with the help of it. The training program will teach you everything from the basics, in a simple and easy-to-understand language. Therefore, you can easily start making money on YouTube.

What can I learn with UtubeCash?

With UtubeCash, you will be able to understand how to create videos, edit videos and market them on YouTube. You will be able to receive effective results with the assistance of this training program. Therefore, you will never have to worry about anything. When you become a subscriber of UtubeCash, you will also be provided with access to one-on-one consultation sessions. These consultation sessions can improve your chances of making more money on YouTube.

What will UtubeCash deliver you?

You should understand what UtubeCash will deliver you, before you go ahead and invest your money to purchase the product. The most important lesson that UtubeCash will teach you is how to make money from YouTube, without investing on marketing. This will assist you to refrain from spending large volumes of money on YouTube marketing campaigns. You will be able to receive the best out of your investment with minimum hassle.

You don't even need to have a website in order to start making money on YouTube with the assistance of UtubeCash. It will teach you the steps that you must follow in order to make money on YouTube without having a website. You can get all the skills that you need for money-making on YouTube and there is no reason for you to worry about anything.

Conclusion

As you can see, UtubeCash is an effective guide, which any person will be able to follow in order to generate a decent profit out of YouTube. Therefore, you are strongly encouraged to focus more attention towards this program and get the best possible results out of it. You will never regret about the results that it can provide to you in the long run and you will appreciate what you get.

Making Money From Home – Part 3

Make Money from Home with Online Surveys

If you are looking for a convenient and a hassle free method to make money online, you can take a look at the online surveys. You don't need to be equipped with any special skills to make a decent amount of money through online surveys. Having a basic understanding on how to use computers and how to access the internet will be more than enough to assist you with achieving positive results. Hence, all individuals who are looking for an effective method to make money online can take a look at them.

What exactly is an online survey?

If you want to make money working from home, you can take a look at the online surveys. But before you do it, you will need to get a better understanding on what exactly they are. Then you will be able to work accordingly and make a decent amount of money at the comfort of your home.

The online surveys can simply be defined as a part of the self-administered surveys. As you already know, the self-administrative surveys are conducted through internet or by post. The opposite of self-administered surveys is administrated surveys, which is being conducted through telephone or face to face.

When you fill an online survey, you will be provided with the questionnaire on the web. Then you will be asked to provide your opinion on a subject of interest. You will be given more than enough time to provide answers to the questionnaire. All you have to be is honest when you fill the questionnaire. Then you will be able to do justice to the survey and provide an excellent assistance for the survey organizer to get his expectations catered. In fact, the overall quality of an online survey depends on the nature of information that you provide. Due to this reason, you are strongly encouraged to provide reliable information when completing the online survey as much as possible.

When you complete the online survey, all the answers that you provide will be sent to the client. However, your individual identity will not be exposed to the client. It is possible to aggregate the survey results by combining multiple responses along with the individuals who took part in it. Usually, all the data collected from the questionnaire will be stored in a database. When the clients want to gain access to the data, they tend to refer to the database. However, your personal data, which is stored in the database will never be exposed to any external entity. On the other hand, they will not be traded or sold without your permission as well. Therefore, you don't need to keep any doubts or second thoughts in mind while you are completing the survey. It can provide you with the level of privacy that you expect to receive.

How can you earn money with online-survey taking?

Now you have a basic understanding of what online surveys are. With that in mind, it is important to understand how to make money. People who conduct surveys are hungry for data. They are always looking forward to get in touch with individuals, who can fill the questionnaires and help them with their research activities. Since it is not an easy task to get people to spend their time and fill in lengthy questionnaires, they tend to make a payment as well. This payment is being made as a token of appreciation. In other words, you spend your time and efforts to go through the questions and answer them. For that, you will be compensated with a decent amount. That's how you will be able to make money with online survey taking.

The online surveys usually go hand in hand with the product tests. In some instances, you will be provided with a dummy product to test. You just need to use that product and write down your honest opinion about it. You will be paid for that as well. Therefore, you must also keep that in your mind when you are looking for an effective method on how to make money working from home with the help of surveys.

Now you must be wondering how to find surveys, which you can complete. Looking for surveys to complete is not something difficult to do. That's because many websites that exist out there on the internet provide people with the opportunity to get their hands on online surveys. You just need to take a look at those websites and get your hands on the best survey sites out of them. Then you will be able to complete surveys according to your specific preferences and make a decent amount of money.

The time you spend with filling online surveys is totally worth. That's because you will be able to get a decent income for the time that is being spent on the job. Therefore, any person can think about going forward with this opportunity. You will never get disappointed with the results you get. You will never regret about it as well. All you have to do is to enjoy the work that you do and the results that you get at the end of the day.

To get the most out of online form filling and to make money working from home, you are encouraged to do your own research and get to know about the best websites that provide the opportunity. Then you will be able to get your hands on the best opportunities out of them and make sure that you don't face any hassle with what you do. This will generate a decent income for you in the long run as well. Since this type of work require minimum knowledge and experience, you can do them without keeping any second thoughts in your mind.

How Much Money Can You Make with Online Surveys?

Are you about to make money working from home? Then you must be looking for how much money you will be able to earn with it. It's not possible to give a direct answer to the question how much money you can make with online surveys? That's because the specific amount of money that you can earn vary based on several factors.

Is completing surveys worth your time?

As the first thing, let's see if completing surveys online is worth your time or not. As mentioned earlier, the amount of money you can earn with online surveys will change on a daily basis. The time you spend on completing online surveys can create a major impact on the specific amount of money that you can earn. Likewise, the nature of surveys can also create an impact on the amount that you can earn.

These factors are within your control. Therefore, you need to take a look at the methods on how you can find surveys, which can help you to earn a decent amount for the time and effort that you spend. Then you will not end up with any disappointments when completing the surveys online.

How many surveys panels should you join?

Some people believe that joining a lot of survey panels can help them to make money online. However, signing up with more survey websites doesn't mean that you can earn hundreds of dollars per month. Instead, you will end up with a loaded email box, which is quite overwhelming.

It is recommended for you to go ahead and sign up with around 5 different survey websites. This is the optimum number of panels that you must sign up with in order to make a decent amount of money. You can begin with 5 panels and see if there is any possibility for you to receive benefits by signing up with more panels in the future. This kind of approach can help you to end up with impressive results in the long run.

Why shouldn't I join to more survey websites?

You need to keep in mind that some of the most prominent survey websites are working with the same market research companies that exist out there in the world. This is the main reason why you will not be able to increase your chances of making more money, by signing up with more survey websites. Even if you are invited, you will not be able to complete the survey. That's because the surveys tend to log your IP address to avoid fraud.

What can you do to earn more with surveys?

As you can see, signing up with more survey websites cannot help you with earning more. It is recommended for you to begin with a couple of websites, which are reputed. Get cash for surveys and Paid surveys are few examples for such websites. You can sign up with these websites and see how they work. Then you can join the other websites and proceed.

Time you need to spend on the survey websites

MAKING MONEY FROM HOME

If you are interested in making a serious amount of money with online survey sites, you will need to invest a considerable amount of time on a daily basis. There are no shortcuts to earn more while completing surveys. However, the time you spend with them is totally worth when compared to the amount that you can earn at the end of the month.

Most of the people tend to spend around 4 hours a day by completing surveys online. If you can work more hours, you should do it as the chances of making more money will increase. But if you are working on surveys for more than 8 hours a day, you need to take precautions. It can lead you towards fatigue and headaches.

What can you do to earn more?

Instead of spending several hours on a daily basis to make money with online surveys, you can select around two survey websites and focus on the completion of surveys. Some people tend to treat the online survey websites as a regular job. When you master the art of completing surveys to make money, you can treat it like your full-time job. Until that, you are encouraged to work on it as your side-hustle.

You can focus on the online surveys during your off days. You can make it a habit to check your emails as the first thing you wake up in the morning. Then you will be able to see the invitations from the survey websites. Or else, you can directly refer to the survey websites that you have signed up with. You must always keep in mind that completing surveys should be a fun-filled experienced and it should not lead you towards any stress.

How much can you earn from surveys?

It is not possible to give a direct answer to this question. That's because the exact amount of money you can earn varies from one survey panel to another. It also varies depending on the surveys that you complete. Some panels tend to make the payments with points, whereas others make the payments directly with cash. Even though the points have a monetary value, it can be quite tricky. Therefore, you need to be aware of it when you are completing online surveys.

The exact amount of money you can earn from a survey depends on the length of the survey and the depth of the survey. You might get $10 from one survey, whereas you will only be provided with $1 on another survey. However, the survey that you have to do to earn $1 will only take 5 minutes, whereas you will have to spend 1 hour to complete the survey that you have to do to earn $10. Technically, completing more of $1 surveys is better than you can earn more money at the end of the hour.

How Do Online Surveys Work and How to Get Paid Using Them

Online surveys are one of the most popular methods available for the people to make money working from home. If you are struggling to earn a decent income by working on your spare time, this is a good opportunity available to grab. All you have to do is to complete the questionnaires at your home and make an earning for it.

Before you start completing online surveys to make money, it is important to have a basic understanding on how they work. Then you will be able to work accordingly and maximize your chances of making more money.

How do online surveys work?

You will be able to find many websites, which offer online surveys for the interested people to complete. However, the way how these surveys work differ from one to another. On the other hand, the way how specific surveys are being used also differ from one to another.

In general, the companies and other similar entities are in need of data to make informed decisions about their future initiatives. For example, a company tends to gather customer data before launching a new product. Then they determine whether the product will be successful among customers. On the other hand, the data company gathers can also contribute towards making appropriate changes product to make it popular and useful for the potential customers.

Out of data collection methods available for the companies, surveys hold a prominent place. However, no person is willing to spend his precious time and complete the surveys to help the companies. As a result, the companies tend to make a payment for the people, in favor of completing the questionnaires and providing them with valuable data. This is how the online surveys work.

How to make money online with surveys?

Now you have a basic understanding about the purpose of online surveys. With that in mind, you can take a look at how you will be able to make money working from home with the assistance of online surveys.

You will be answering the questionnaires that the companies provide with the objective of gathering data. You need to be honest when providing answers to them. Then you need to go ahead and submit your answers. In return, you will be provided with a payment. Completing online surveys is simple as that. You don't need to have any special skills to do it and make money at the comfort of your home.

Signing up with online surveys websites

To begin with, you can sign up with the online survey websites. However, you need to be vigilant at the time of signing up. That's because there are many scam websites on the internet and you will need to take appropriate measures to stay away from them. You should not sign up with any website that requests for a large upfront fee.

At the time of signing up to a website that provides online surveys, you will have to answer a series of questions. These questions will be about yourself and the lifestyle that you follow. These questions are asked from you because the website needs to provide you with surveys that match with you. Therefore, you must be honest when providing answers to these questions. On the other hand, this will help you to get interesting surveys to complete, based on your preferences.

Should I provide my sensitive information?

When you are signing up with online surveys websites to make money working from home, you will have to provide your sensitive information. They include your name, your address, your email address, your contact number and your age. This is applicable even for the most prominent websites that provide surveys, such as Get Cash for Surveys and Paid Surveys for Cash.

The companies that offer surveys to the websites are looking for the best fitting individuals to complete them. Otherwise, they will not be able to end up with accurate information. This is the main reason why they ask for your personal and sensitive information. For example, when you enter your age, you will be provided with surveys that match perfectly well with your age. A teenager would not want to complete a survey about senior care facilities. If you don't want to end up with such questionnaires, you need to provide your honest information.

You don't need to think twice before you feed your personal information to a reputed website. Your personal and sensitive information is protected at all times. Therefore, you don't need to worry about anything.

What happens when you complete the paid survey?

When you are completing the online survey, you will have to answers to the questions. All the answers that you provide will be submitted to the company that provides the questionnaire. You are not the only person who completes the survey. All the gathered data will be analyzed by the company that provides the survey. Then the company will take appropriate measures in order to improve their products, services or the business processes.

The next stage associated with online surveys is quite technical. In fact, the companies are looking forward to finding the cheapest place in order to produce the products or sell the products. The data that the company gathers from surveys provide a great assistance when making decisions. However, you need to provide your honest opinion when completing the surveys, so that you will be able to provide assistance for the companies to make better decisions.

How will you get paid?
Some websites that offer online surveys pay with cash whereas others pay with coins. You can convert the coins to cash at a later stage. When you keep on completing surveys, you will be able to

make more money. Then you will be able to withdraw them to your bank account or any other online wallet such as PayPal.

Top Online Survey Sites

When you want to make money working from home, you can take a look at the paid surveys online. To engage with paid surveys, you must take a look at the websites that provide you with the surveys. many such websites are available on the internet, but all of them are not in a position to provide you with an excellent service as you expect. That's why we thought of providing you with a list of the best online surveys websites. If you want to make money online, you can take a look at these websites and you will be able to receive impressive results.

Savvy Connect

Savvy Connect is one of the most innovative platforms available for you to complete surveys and get paid for them. To begin with, you will need to install the app on your PC, mobile or any other device, which you can use to connect to the internet. Then this app will work in the background and gather required information.

To increase your earnings with Savvy Connect, you can recommend it to others. For every person who installs this app, you will be able to earn around $5 to $15. There is no minimum payout to withdraw and you will be able to receive a check payment upon request.

SurveySavvy

SurveySavvy has received a lot of attention in the recent past as well. That's because the website provides people with access to the highest paying surveys. You will be able to earn somewhere in between $1 to $20 by completing the surveys available on this website. Therefore, it can be considered as a website that you must use.

SurveySavvy also provides additional payments for the referrals that you bring in. When you bring in more referrals, your chances to make money online will increase. That's because you will be able to earn in between $1 to $2 for every survey that your referrals complete. Moreover, you can earn around $0.5 to $1 via the indirect referrals as well. No minimum payout is needed for you to request for a withdrawal on this website. You will be able to get funds via a check.

MindSwarms

Among the online surveys websites, MindSwarms is another highly discussed option available for you to consider. You will be able to complete highly paying surveys, which can provide you with up to $50 per survey on this website. Therefore, you can engage with it without keeping any doubts or second thoughts in mind. To earn this amount, you will not have to complete lengthy surveys. It is possible for you to complete a survey with just 7 questions and earn $50.

The MindSwarms website has an interactive survey completion mechanism as well. You will be provided with the questions on the interface. These questions are determined based on your profile and demographics. You will be provided with 7 such questions to answer on this website. At the end of the questionnaire, you can receive the payout. MindSwarms makes the payments through PayPal.

Parent Speak

Parent Speak is an online surveys website that is available for the parents to use. If you are a parent who is looking forward to make money working from home, you can take a look at this website. Parent Speak is backed up by C+R Research, which is a marketing firm based in Chicago. This is not just a survey website. As a parent, you will be able to connect with other parents and discuss many things through this platform.

Most of the surveys that you can find in Parent Speak are linked with follow-up questions. Therefore, it will take a considerable amount of time for you to complete them. They cover a variety of topics, which are related to the parents, such as clothing, entertainment, food and electronics. You can earn around $20 to $50 by completing the surveys available on this website. Payments will be made through check.

PineCone Research

If you are looking for an exclusive online survey panel, you can take a look at PineCone Research. That's because not all people can sign up for accounts on this website. You will only be able to create an account in PineCone Research if you are invited. In addition, you need to keep in mind that PineCone Research has specific quotas for invitations as well. If the quota is reached, you will not be able to create an account on PineCone Research, even if you have an invitation.

Previously, PineCone Research made a flat rate payment of $3 for every survey that you took. However, the things have slightly changed now and you will be able to earn more or less depending on the nature of the survey that you take. You need to have a minimum amount of at least $3 in your account to initiate the withdrawal. Payouts in PineCone Research will be made through Visa gift cards, direct deposits and checks.

Nielsen Digital Voice Research Panel

Nielsen Digital Voice Research Panel is a survey website that is backed up by a market research group. The entire program was developed with the intention of gathering information related to audience size and audio composition of the television programs that are being telecasted in United States. Now Nielsen Digital Voice Research Panel has increased the scope. As a result, you will be able to discover a lot of additional surveys available in the website.

You can sign up with Nielsen Digital Voice Research Panel for free. Then you need to install the free app that they give to your computer or any other device. The app will work on the background and collect appropriate data. At the end of every month, you will be able to enter to the $10,000 sweepstakes, where 400 lucky winners walk away with amazing prices. If you are not making money directly, you can consider this website.

BAD ONLINE SURVEY SITES THAT YOU MUST REFRAIN FROM

When you want to make money working from home, you tend to take a look at the online surveys websites. That's because there is a high possibility for you to make a decent amount of money by spending minimum effort. However, all the survey websites that promote the ability to make money online cannot deliver guaranteed results.

If you are about to complete surveys online, you are encouraged to have a clear understanding about these websites. Then you can take appropriate steps to refrain from those websites. Here is a list of bad online survey sites that you need to refrain from.

- Toluna

Toluna is a website that provides you with the opportunity to test products at the comfort of your home and write reviews on them. However, the rewarding system that you can find on this website is somewhat poor. You will not be compensated enough for the time that you spend in order to complete surveys on this website. On the other hand, the surveys that you complete on this website aren't worth very much as well.

When you create an account on Toluna, you will notice that your email inbox is getting bombarded with notifications and emails. These emails don't have any value and it will be a big headache. You will be earning points for the completion of surveys on Toluna.

However, you will need to use those points within a period of one year upon earning. Otherwise, you will lose access to the points.

- One Poll

One Poll promotes itself as a great little website, which can help you to earn money during your coffee breaks. But when you sign up with this website, you will notice that it is not interesting as it sounds. You will not be able to earn a lot of money when you complete the surveys. In fact, completion of a survey will only provide you with $0.10 to $0.15. The time you spend on the work is not worth when compared to the results that you get.

In some surveys that you complete in One Poll, you will be able to receive the rewards as prize draws. You will not be able to get any money from these surveys. The prize draws doesn't guarantee monetary prizes to you as well. Therefore, you might have to walk away with nothing. When you are completing online surveys on this website, you will need to earn at least 40 GBP before you can request for a withdrawal. With the amount of money that you can make on the site, it will take a considerable amount of time for the withdrawals.

- Global Test Market

Global Test Market is an established website, which you can use to make money through the completion of surveys. You will be able to get surveys to complete on a daily basis after creating an account on this website. However, most of those surveys are broken. This will make you waste a considerable amount of time when completing them.

Before you start filling the questionnaire, you will have to go through a screening process as well. This screening process is relatively long and it will take a couple of minutes. Some surveys available on this website will also take ages to complete. However, you will not be able to receive a decent amount of money for the time you spend to complete them. Even though Global Test Market records all your personal information at the time of creating the account, you will notice that you are getting completely irrelevant surveys at times.

- UK My Survey

UK My Survey is a great platform available for the people in UK to complete surveys and make money. However, there are some drawbacks associated with this website as well. The biggest drawback out of them is constant screen outs. This can lead you towards a lot of frustrating moments when you complete the surveys. In addition to that, you will be able to discover many broken surveys on the website as well.

You will notice that most of the surveys that are available to complete on this website are similar. If you ignore this fact and complete the surveys, you will come across issues with the payment. In fact, you will not be able to receive a payment for the duplicate surveys.

- Pinecone Research

Pinecone Research is another popular online surveys website. If you are looking forward to make money working from home through this website, you need to take a quick look at the drawbacks linked with it. The entire website has a somewhat confusing design. You will get confused when you are trying to access the reward center. In fact, you will have to struggle a lot when you are trying to locate the withdrawal button for the very first time when using the website.

You will also be asked to enter your user name and password when you are trying to complete a survey at all times. This can also lead you towards a lot of pain. Only one person at your home will be allowed to create a Pinecone Research account. The sign-up process is quite complicated as well. Completion of surveys is the only method available for you to make money on Pinecone Research. There is no friend referral scheme.

Now you are aware of some of the worst online survey websites available on the internet. You must take appropriate steps to stay away from these websites. If you take a closer look at these websites, you will notice some common aspects in between them as well. Therefore, you are encouraged to keep your hands away from the online surveys websites that come with such features. Then you can get the most for the amount that you spend with completing online surveys.

Making Money From Home – Part 4

How to Make Money from Home as a Virtual Assistant

Out of the opportunities available for you to make money working from home, becoming a virtual assistant has received a lot of attention. That's because you will be able to provide a service that you are familiar with by working as a virtual assistant and make a considerable amount of money at the end of the day.

Do I need to have experience?

Even if you are not an expert in a specific area, you can still try to become a virtual assistant. You can quickly catch up the things and make money online. In fact, you will get paid to learn when you are working as a virtual assistant. This will help you to grow your business and improve your chances of making a solid income.

How to become a virtual assistant without any experience?

When you are looking forward to become a virtual assistant without any experience, you are encouraged to do a bit of research on the market. You can see what other people do as virtual assistants in order to make money. Then you will be able to figure out something, which you can also do. Then you can follow it and make money working from home.

You shouldn't aim to make thousands of dollars from the very first month you work as a virtual assistant. Instead, you must aim for a slow beginning. For example, you can help someone with doing social media management. Or else, you can research on a subject matter and provide recommendations.

Looking for your very first client

When it comes to freelancing, looking for your very first client is the most difficult thing to do. This is applicable for the individuals who make the decision to work as virtual assistants as well. You will not have any idea at all on how to find a client.

In this kind of situation, the freelancing websites can help you with. You can take a look at the freelancing websites such as Freelancer and Upwork. In addition, the lesser known websites such as People per Hour can also provide you with impressive results when looking for a virtual assistant. Then you can locate the clients who look for virtual assistants and then offer your services to them.

Offering the services that clients want

Clients want many types of virtual assistant related services. It is better if you can have a basic understanding about those services before you begin. Then you will be able to make appropriate decisions when applying for jobs online.

The virtual assistants will have to work on freelance writing, eBook writing, guest blogging, blog management, marketing campaign management, webinars, social media scheduling, social media management, email management, copywriting, researching, fact checking and many more. You can narrow down your focus on a few of these services, especially when you are looking for your very first client. When you gain experience while working as a virtual assistant, you can think about offering more services.

Create a portfolio or a website

If you want to ensure your success in the future as a virtual assistant, you are encouraged to create a portfolio or a website. On the website, you can highlight your previous experiences in working as a virtual assistant. The primary objective of creating a portfolio or a website is to increase your credibility as a virtual assistant. This can contribute a lot towards your future success.

You can also add some packages to your website. Then you will be able to provide more information to the potential clients, who are willing to get the services that you offer. In addition, you need to get some client testimonials on your website. You can reach to your previous clients and tell them that you have created a new website and you are looking forward to improve it with some reviews. Then the clients will go ahead and leave reviews about the services that you offered.

You must also get a contact form for the website that you create. Otherwise, you will miss out a lot of opportunities available out there to grab. The contact form can help the potential clients to get in touch with you and hire you for their virtual assistant tasks.

How to determine your rates

It has been identified that most of the virtual assistants get confused when they are determining their rates. Some virtual assistants tend to charge per hour whereas others charge a flat rate. At the beginning, it is better if you can charge your clients on an hourly basis. That's because you will not be able to make a clear estimation on how much time it will consume for you to get the job done.

When you have some experience in working as a virtual assistant, you will know how much time it will cost for you to get a specific task done. In that kind of situation, you can simply switch to a flat rate. Then you will be able to increase the amount of money that you make at the end of the day as well. However, your rates should be reasonable for the clients.

Conclusion

Now you know how to make money online by working as a virtual assistant. With that in mind, you can go ahead and follow the steps. It is an easy and a hassle free method that any person can follow to make a decent amount of money at the comfort of home. You can also keep on learning new skills and it will help you to take your work to the next level.

If you dream of becoming a successful virtual assistant in the future, you are encouraged not to stop learning. Then you can stay up to date and polish your skills at all times to deliver a better service to your clients.

How to Become a Virtual Assistant (Getting the Skills Needed)

You don't need to be equipped with any special skills to become a virtual assistant. But if you go ahead and try to become a virtual assistant without having an understanding of even the basics, you will not be able to make money online. As a result, you will get frustrated and you will tend to give up. Therefore, all the individuals who are looking forward to make money working from home as virtual assistants are strongly encouraged to learn the basic skills that are needed to ensure their success in the long run.

Here is a list of some basic skills that you must have to become a successful virtual assistant. We will also let you know how you will be able to get these skills and make money online with minimum hassle.

Learn how to plan and strategize

As the first thing, you must learn how to plan and strategize. You need to focus on the principles and take your time to craft a plan. You can easily get yourself engaged with the work that is available in front of you. But you should also determine what will happen tomorrow or in next week. When you proceed without a proper plan, there is a high possibility for you to feel overwhelmed. This can eventually make you give up.

You can create a plan for the next year, next day and the next week. Then you must follow the plan. If you notice that you are finding difficulties when you follow the plan, you are strongly encouraged to take a look at the plan again and make appropriate changes in it. This will help you to overcome the frustrating moments that you might face in the future.

Prioritize all the revenue generating tasks

When you are working as a virtual assistant, you are strongly encouraged to prioritize all the revenue generating tasks. It is better if you can learn the lessons from someone who learnt it in the hard way. When you don't focus more on the tasks that can generate higher revenues, you will suffer financially. This can even force you to go out of business.

Virtual assistants have millions of things to do. However, all those things cannot help you earn a decent amount of money. Due to this reason, you must focus only on the revenue generating tasks. If you can prioritize them, you will be able to focus on the activities that make money revenue to you. This will make you feel happy about the work that you do as a virtual assistant as well.

Don't Multitask

Multitasking is a smart skill to have. But when you are working as a virtual assistant, you must think twice before you multitask. That's because multitasking is in a position to lead you towards some serious issues in the long run.

Assume that it will take just one hour for you to get something done. But when you multitask, it will take around 8 hours for you to do it. This will create a negative impression on the mind of your client, as he knows how much time is needed to get the job done. In fact, your client will think that you are an inefficient virtual assistant. Multitasking can often give life to quality related issues as well.

To overcome this issue, you are encouraged to focus on batching. You can take a look at the tasks that you want to achieve and create batches. Then you will be able to prioritize the batches and focus on what's important.

Learn how to communicate effectively

Effective communication is an important skill that every virtual assistant must have. It is worth to invest your time and get this skill. Then you will not walk away with any disappointment in the future. You should be clear and concise when you are communicating something to your client. It can be about the job that you do or a payment.

While you try to improve the communication skills, you must also keep in mind that listening plays a major role in here. In fact, listening is responsible for around 50% of the communication capabilities that you have. Therefore, you should learn how to listen and how to speak properly. This will make you a better person with the sales. In addition, you will be a better person when resolving conflicts as well. In the long run, you will be able to attend to the client requirements and cater them in an effective manner.

Develop the sales skills that you have

Last but not least, you need to take appropriate steps to develop the sales skills that you have. You might not be working as a sales assistant for the clients. But still, you must promote yourself to the clients to win projects. This is where your sales skills will come into play. You must have the ability to promote your skillset to the potential clients, who are looking for the service offered by virtual assistants.

You can be yourself while improving the sales skills. This will help you to develop a unique identity. Then you can communicate the value that you have. This will tempt the clients to go ahead and recruit you for the virtual assistant tasks.

Conclusion

As you can see, a variety of skills are needed for a person to become a virtual assistant. You can take a moment to see whether you are equipped with these skills or not. If you are not equipped these skills, you are strongly encouraged to focus on them. Then you will be able to sharpen your skills and improve your ability to work as a better virtual assistant.

- Main Keyword is "Make Money Working From Home,"
- Second Keyword is "Make Money Online"
- Third Keyword is whatever the category is such as "Online Surveys"

How Much Money Does a Virtual Assistant Make

Are you planning to become a virtual assistant? Then you are about to make one of the best decisions in your life. But before you become a virtual assistant, it is important to have a basic understanding on how much money you will be able to make. Then you can determine whether the time you spend to become a virtual assistant is worth it or not.

What factors contribute towards the amount that I can earn?

Becoming a virtual assistant to make money working from home is something that you can try with minimum skills. However, it is better if you can develop your skills along with time. That's because the amount you can make increases along with your skill profile. Here are some of the most prominent factors, which can contribute towards the amount of money that you will be able to earn when working as a virtual assistant.

     Education – If you have relevant educational qualifications, your chances of making more money will increase.

     Years of experience – The years of experience that you have in the respective field can help you to make more money as a virtual assistant.

     Complexity of work – If you are working on a complex project, you will usually be paid with a higher rate. Lack of expertise available to get the job done is one of the most prominent reasons behind the above-mentioned fact. On the other hand, the clients are also aware of the complexity and they tend to reward you for the additional efforts you spend.

Supply and demand – When the supply available for the type of work that you do is less, you will be able to demand more. But when the supply is high, you cannot demand more because there are virtual assistants, who are willing to offer the same service at a lower price tag.

Supervision required – If you are capable of getting the job done under minimal supervision, you will be able to earn more. Otherwise, the client will have to spend more time and effort on supervising your work as well.

Work conditions – When you are working under strenuous conditions, you will be able to receive a better compensation for the work that you do.

Does my country create an impact on the amount I can earn?

When you make money online, you will notice that people who live in different parts of the world are not being paid equally. In fact, your geographical location can create a tremendous impact on the amount that you can earn as a virtual assistant as well.

For example, if you are from United States, you will be able to get a better hourly rate when working as a virtual assistant. But if you are from an Asian country, such as Philippines or India, you will be provided with a lower hourly rate. In other words, the average hourly rating of a virtual assistant from USA is around $15, whereas the average hourly rating of a virtual assistant from Philippines is around $3. When it comes to countries like Mexico, the hourly rate is average, at around $7 per hour.

You need to keep this fact in your mind when determining the amount of money that you will be able to earn as a virtual assistant.

The amount you can earn depends on your skills

There is no straightforward answer to the question, "How much money can I earn as a virtual assistant?" That's because the amount you can earn depends on the nature of work that you do. If you can keep this fact in mind, you can easily increase your chances of making more money as a virtual assistant. It will not be possible for you to do it at once. But you can have a slow start and then proceed along with time. Then you will be able to end up with outstanding results.

If you want to make more money by working as a virtual assistant, you are encouraged to do something unique at all times. You will need to contribute towards the growth of your client's business as well. Then you will be provided with a high hourly rate. Even if you are not being offered with a higher hourly rate, you can humbly request and go for it.

Are hourly rates better?

Some virtual assistants are being paid with an hourly rate, whereas others get a flat rate. When you consider the amount of money that you can make as a virtual assistant, you will take a look at these choices as well.

When you are beginning to work as a virtual assistant, it is better to go ahead with a flat rate. That's because you will have to spend a considerable amount of extra time to get the job done. It is not reasonable to charge heavily from the client for your learning. Then you can switch to hourly rates and provide the best service for the amount that is being spent by the client. When you are working for an hourly rate, you have better chances of negotiating your rates as well.

What can I do to increase my income?

When you make money working from home as a virtual assistant, you will wonder about the steps, which you can take to increase your income. That's where your skills come into play. If you have an excellent skill set, your chances of making more money as a virtual assistant will increase. You need to be an expert in the area of specialization. In addition, you need to acquire rare skills.

You should also learn how to solve problems. Then you can volunteer and solve the problems that businesses face. This will help you to get paid for the service that you offer. Hence, you can increase the amount of money that you earn per month.

What Tasks Virtual Assistants Do To Make Money

Virtual assistants do many type of work in order to make money. If you are willing to become a virtual assistant, you must be curious to get to know about the activities that virtual assistants do in order to make money. Here is a list of some of the most prominent methods out of them. You can go through the list and see if there are any methods that you can follow in order to make money working from home. If there are, you can follow it and earn a decent income without spending a lot of efforts.

Creating content for social media

Businesses in today's world manage their own social media accounts. However, most of the companies don't want to go through the hassle of uploading content for social media on their own. Apart from uploading content, they have to spend a lot of time to create content as well. As a result, they tend to seek the assistance of a virtual assistant.

When you are working as a virtual assistant to make money online, you can create content for the social media campaigns. To do that, you will have to conduct researches on the interesting articles on the internet and come up with content. On the other hand, you will have to work on quote graphics, images and reference article links as well. By paying special attention towards content, you will be able to help the businesses to keep their social media profiles up to date with appropriate content.

Brainstorming headlines and managing the blog editorial calendar

The editorial calendar can simply be defined as a plan, which defines the schedule of all the upcoming blog posts, which will be published. As a virtual assistant, you will be able to manage this as well. You will have to brainstorm topic ideas and headlines, which will be appealing to the businesses and target audiences. This will help the websites to boost the rankings that they have on the search engines.

Formatting the posts on WordPress

WordPress is the most common CMS used by websites that exist out there in the internet. When the website owners get content written, they come across the need to paste them on the website. However, it will not be an easy thing to do. They often come across a series of challenges when pasting content in the WordPress websites. As a virtual assistant, you will have to help them.

In here, your primary responsibility would be to edit and format content. You need to make sure that the content is being published on the WordPress website appropriately, without any errors. WordPress is extremely easy to learn. Therefore, you don't need to go through any struggles to work with it and get your work done. If you are new to freelancing, this is a good opportunity available to make money online.

Proofreading the articles and blog posts

Proofreading the articles and blog posts can be considered as another highly in demand opportunity available for the virtual assistants who want to make money working from home. Before you start working on this, you need to keep in mind that you should be fluent in the language that you are working with. Otherwise, it will not be possible for you to detect the mistakes and correct them. In other words, you will fail to provide the service that you are supposed to offer.

You will get draft blog posts and articles in many different types. You will need to go through those articles and blog posts to locate the mistakes. If there are any mistakes, you should go ahead and correct them. Then you can send to the clients. Or else, you can directly upload them to the websites and blogs. If you are good with a language, this is one of the best jobs that you can take to make money as a virtual assistant.

Providing customer support

Similar to social media content, many businesses that exist out there in the world tend to outsource customer support as well. The ability to get customer support services at a lower price tag holds a prominent place out of them. As a virtual assistant, you will be able to work on these customer support work. All the questions, feedback and inquiries will be outsourced to the virtual assistants. Depending on the nature of questions and inquiries, you will have to work alone, or along with another team.

You will have to respond to all the incoming concerns in correspondence. You need to be accurate with the information that you provide. You might have to respond to them in the form of emails, live chat or via calls. You will also need to be prompt with your responses. Then you can ensure maximum customer satisfaction.

Creating landing pages

When businesses want to sell products or services, they create landing pages. However, many businesses are not interested in creating these landing pages on their own. Instead, they prefer to get the help of virtual assistants for the creation of landing pages. You can work on them and help the businesses with boosting their sales volumes.

You need to have basic web designing skills and knowledge to create landing pages. Then you will be able to create the best landing pages, which can help the businesses with increasing the sales volume. To make your life easy with creating landing pages, you can find many templates as well. You can take a look at these templates and select the best ones out of them to take your initiatives to the next level.

Conclusion

Now you are aware of some work that virtual assistants do in order to make money from home. If you are good with any of these, you can get started right away. There is a high demand for such work as well and you don't need to worry about anything.

Top Money Making Virtual Assistant Jobs

Virtual assistant jobs are highly in demand. You can also think about becoming a virtual assistant, so that you can make money working from home, without any hassle. But before you get into the virtual assistant jobs, you need to understand what type of work that people do as virtual assistants in order to make money. Then you can select the most appropriate type of work out of those opportunities and make money online. This will provide you with a decent income in the long run and you will not have to worry too much about anything.

Below mentioned are some of the highest paid jobs that virtual assistants can do.

Social media managers

From the recent studies, it has been identified that the total amount of money that companies spend on social media has been increased by 70% during the past year. This has given life to many opportunities, which virtual assistants can grab. Even though the companies have a demand for getting their social media related work done, they prefer to outsource the work to virtual assistants due to the convenience associated with it.

When you work as a social media manager, you will have to do everything from opening up social media accounts under the company name to responding the customer inquiries that come into the social media account. You need to make sure that you keep the social media profiles up to date by uploading relevant information. You need to come up with an effective content creation strategy to end up with the best possible results. In addition, you will have to do researches to gather ideas on trends, which can be used to take the social media marketing campaigns to the next level.

SEO manager

In a similar way to social media marketing, you also have many opportunities to grab as an SEO manager. Since all the businesses in today's world are concerned about securing top rankings in search engine results, there is a high demand for the SEO managers as well. But before you work as an SEO manager, you need to learn the basics of SEO and the techniques that can deliver positive results. Then you will be able to end up as a successful virtual assistant.

While you are working as a SEO manager, you will need to develop and update the SEO strategy of the business. You will need to update the website accordingly as well. To ensure the search engine rankings, you will have to conduct keyword researches. A variety of SEO tools are available for you to use when you are working on a SEO campaign. You need to be aware of what the best tools out of them are and how to get the most out of those tools. Then you will be able to do competitor analysis and help your client to get the website ranked on search engines.

Content writing

Content plays a major role behind the marketing campaigns that you can find out there in the world. As a result, there is a high demand for the content writers as well. You can also become a content writer when you want to make money online as a virtual assistant. You can write content in many different languages. But you need to make sure that you are familiar with the language that you are working on. In other words, you need to be an expert in the language to provide an outstanding service to the clients.

As a content writer, you will need to work on article and blog post creation. After creating the articles and blog posts, you will have to publish them on the internet as well. You can either publish the articles or blog posts that you create on the websites of the clients, or else, you can think about publishing them on article directories. While you create the articles, you need to pay special attention towards backlink creation as well. In addition, you will come across the need to compose compelling newsletters, press releases and other types of viral content.

General virtual assistants

Most of the virtual assistants are being hired in the online world for general purposes. If you don't have any special skills, you can think about becoming a general virtual assistant. Even though the amount of money that you will be able to earn as a general virtual assistant is relatively low, it is not disappointing. You will be able to get a decent amount of money with the nature of work that you do. The time you spend is totally worth and you will be impressed with the amount of money that you can earn with the skills that you have.

As a general virtual assistant, you will need to work on payroll duties and bookkeeping. Or else, you will have to work as a receptionist by answering calls and checking messages. If you have basic technical skills, you can think about working on technical tasks. They include data entry, database building and managing CRM. You can also work on customer management. In here, you will need to write and send invoices to the clients, send appropriate emails to the clients according to customer concerns and organize technical support tickets.

Conclusion

Now you know what types of work that people do as virtual assistants to make money online. All these work opportunities pay you with a decent payout. Therefore, you don't need to worry too much about the time that you spend on these activities. The clients who are looking for virtual assistants under these areas are generous and they know all the hard work that people spend in order to get the work done. Therefore, you will be able to get an excellent amount of money, which is totally worth the side hustle.

ABOUT THE AUTHOR

Paul D. Kings is a Software Engineer, Father, husband, and self-published author. He likes to write about selling and making money online. Paul has been selling on eBay and Amazon since 2007.

MAKING MONEY FROM HOME

Free Gift Offer

Free Training

How to Earn a 6-Figure Side-Income Online

www.ingramcontent.com/pod-product-compliance
Lightning Source LLC
Chambersburg PA
CBHW030637220526
45463CB00004B/1550